*"This book will keep you three
steps ahead of the devil! Amazing
revelation of our victory!"*

—Sid Roth, Host, *It's Supernatural!*

UNMASKING THE DEVIL

DEVIL

STRATEGIES TO DEFEAT ETERNITY'S GREATEST ENEMY

JOHN RAMIREZ

DESTINY IMAGE® PUBLISHERS, INC.
P.O. Box 310, Shippensburg, PA 17257-0310
"Promoting Inspired Lives."

This book and all other Destiny Image and Destiny Image Fiction books are available at Christian bookstores and distributors worldwide.

Cover design by Terry Clifton

For more information on foreign distributors, call 717-532-3040.
Reach us on the Internet: www.destinyimage.com.

ISBN 13 TP: 978-0-7684-0890-4
ISBN 13 eBook: 978-0-7684-0891-1

For Worldwide Distribution, Printed in the U.S.A.
3 4 5 6 7 8 / 19 18 17 16 15

Acknowledgements

For I am not ashamed of the gospel of Christ, for it is the power of God to salvation for everyone who believes, for the Jew first and also for the Greek.
—ROMANS 1:16 (NKJV)

First and foremost I would like to thank and give all the glory, honor, and praise to my Lord and Savior Jesus Christ for giving me this opportunity to write my second book, *Unmasking the Devil*, as this could not have been done without Him. I thank God for making me a bondservant.

One thing I always reflect on is that He is the God of second chances, as in my demonic, devil-worshipping days I used to live in a community that had 179 buildings; I thank God that out of those 179 buildings, Jesus Christ knew my address. Grace and mercy were shone upon me that night and I was set free.

I thank Jesus for the divine appointment in bringing Raoul Davis and Leticia Gomez of Ascendant Group into my life, for this wonderful connection, and for allowing Raoul to tune in that morning to a Christian TV show featuring my story. I am blessed that God prompted his heart to contact me. Raoul is a true man of God and a man who is real and genuine in his own life. I have been very blessed to know him.

I send my deepest appreciation and thanks to Destiny Image and the staff for allowing me to be part of a precious family and such an awesome legacy. I am grateful and thankful for a lifetime.

I also want to send my love and appreciation to the many people of TBN, *The 700 Club*, Church Channel, End Churchianity, and also talk blog radio programs such as Omegaman Radio with Shannon Davis, Watchmen Radio with Richard Keltner, Eternal Planner with Rob Rennie, and 1 on One with Damon Davis. These are amazing ministries, and I am humbled to have the opportunity to be a part of these special ministries in Jesus' name.

Special thanks to the many churches that I have been privileged to minister in. I am grateful to God for these precious open doors.

I want to thank God for my spiritual covering, Champions Ministries in Orlando, Florida, for being such a vital part, not only of my ministry, but also of my personal life. Apostles Alexander and Sandra, thank you for being so good to me and genuine in your walk with the Lord.

I am beyond grateful to be sitting in Times Square Church for the past twelve years and for being under such an awesome ministry that sustains me spiritually. I am always grateful for the three years I was blessed to be mentored by Pastor David Wilkerson. I miss you, Pastor Dave, and one day I will see you again.

I am deeply grateful for Denise Loffredo, for being such an amazing woman of God and taking up the challenge of typing out this precious book and handling the spiritual warfare that came with it. A special thanks to Denise.

I want to thank Angie Kiesling; she is my best friend and my editor. I thank God for her ministry, The Editorial Attic (editorialattic .com). She did an amazing job, just as she did with my first book, *Out of the Devil's Cauldron*. Thank you, Angie, once again.

A special thanks to Brother Shannon Davis of Omegaman Radio. I thank God for his ministry and for bringing us together to destroy the kingdom of darkness through spiritual warfare and deliverance; for us teaming up together, and for collaborating with me to create an incredible chapter in this book to set the captives free. You are a special brother in Christ for life.

To my daughter, Amanda, whom I love with all my heart. You have grown to be a beautiful young lady. I am privileged and feel special and humbled to be your dad. I know that God is going to do incredible things through your life. You are special in every way. I say this once again: out of all the daughters in the world, I thank God every day that He gave me you.

I thank God, the Lord Jesus Christ, for giving me such a special mom, whom I love with all my heart. She is a gift from God. Having a mom like her is like finding a precious pearl.

My brothers, George and Stock, you are precious and awesome in every way possible. I am so blessed to have you as brothers. I see the hand of God upon your lives.

I am amazed at the blessings of God for giving me jewels on the earth: precious Israelites, Jewish Messianic brothers. I have an incredible love for Israel, deeper than the love I have for my own country, Puerto Rico, which I love as well. Precious men of God such as Jeff Kruh, Alan Binger, and Brother David Berkowitz (the Son of Hope) have taught me in a supernatural way to see the Word of God through Jewish eyes. I also thank Nate Binger for an incredible website. I am indebted to the Jewish people for giving us Yeshua, the Savior. I thank God for these precious men.

I am doing a life sentence with Jesus Christ, and I want no parole. Thank you, Jesus.

Contents

A Note from the Author

"I'm here on the ground with my nose in it since the whole thing began. I've nurtured every sensation man's been inspired to have. I cared about what he wanted and I never judged him. Why? Because I never rejected him. In spite of all his imperfections, I'm a fan of man! I'm a humanist. Maybe the last humanist. Who in their right mind, Kevin, could possibly deny the Twentieth Century was entirely mine?

"Don't get too cocky, my boy. No matter how good you are, don't ever let them see you coming. That's the gaffe, my friend. You gotta keep yourself small. Innocuous. Be the little guy. You know, the nerd...the leper... the sh*t-kickin' serf. Look at me: underestimated from day one. You'd never think I was a master of the universe, now would ya?"

—Al Pacino, portraying the character John Milton

If I didn't tell you who this character is supposed to be, and you just looked at the face value of this quote, you might think these statements are logical. Unfortunately, anyone falling for this type of logic is susceptible to Satan.

In the film *The Devil's Advocate* (Warner Bros., 1997), Keanu Reeves portrays Kevin Lomax, a Southern attorney with good morals, but an obsession with winning. John Milton invites Lomax to join Milton's law firm in New York, but then Milton puts Lomax in increasingly "grayer" legal scenarios where Lomax's moral judgment is compromised for wealth. Ultimately, these cases prove to be a test for Lomax as, at the end of the film, John Milton reveals himself to be Satan. As Milton so famously points out, "Vanity is my favorite sin; it is the gateway to all others."

While *The Devil's Advocate* is a work of fiction, imagine meeting a real-life Kevin Lomax, an individual who worked under Satan for many years and then finally pulled away and got a fresh start. Now imagine this person being willing to unmask Satan's tactics and offer both believers of Jesus Christ and the rest of the world the inside scoop on how Satan tries to lure humanity in—and why he has been so masterful at fooling billions of people over time. Imagine this person offering you the keys to defeat Satan's attacks and arming individuals with the tools they need to overcome Satan once and for all. Imagine no longer. My name is John Ramirez, and to quote the rapper Lil Wayne, "I've been to hell and back; I can show you vouchers."

Every word of my story is true and, what's more, it's a message that needs to be heard, now more than ever. People are eager to understand, not only the role of Satan in the modern world but how to combat him. The book you're holding will do just that. If you've ever doubted the power of Jesus Christ, even for a moment, after hearing my story I am hopeful you'll never do so again.

In my first book, I told the story of how I was trained to be the third-ranked high priest of a Satanic cult in New York

City—casting powerful witchcraft spells and controlling entire spiritual regions. But what started as a long spiral into the underworld ended, thankfully, in a miraculous encounter with Jesus Christ that changed the course of my life. I preach and speak from experiences that 99.9 percent of believers have never been exposed to. I've been in the enemy's camp, and I'm a defector.

People from all ethnic backgrounds dabble in the occult and fall victim to this Satanic underworld. Many of them think it is innocent and, trust me, it is anything but. People often get lured in because many of these cults claim to be based in part off of Christianity, or they promise answers on how to get closer to God. People get sent down a road where they lose themselves, fall under the influence of Satan, and never see the way out. With God's grace, I happen to be one of the rare individuals who made it out.

My hope is not only to help Christians learn how to expose and combat Satan, but to help those who are stuck find the pathway out. Within these pages, I share the teachings I have shared with thousands across the world to inspire them to live sanctified lives, fulfill their God-given destiny, and ensure that their soul spends eternity with God.

It's a message that needs to be told, and now more than ever.

OBITUARY

DEAD MAN RAISED TO NEW LIFE

New York, NY—On October 27, 1999

John Ramirez spiritually passed away late at night on his bed in the Bronx, New York. John was born in Puerto Rico and immigrated to the Bronx with his family as a child. He was the father of one daughter. John became the third-ranked devil worshiper in New York City in the spiritual realms of Santeria, Spiritualism, and Palo Mayombe. He was an evangelist for the dark side for twenty-five years and recruited many to "the religion." John enjoyed dominating the spiritual realm against Christians, the Church, and many other religions. In his Satanic mind, if he could control the region, he could control the people. He came conquering like his daddy, the devil: to kill, to steal, and to destroy many. But on the same night he "died" in the Bronx, he was born again—raised up a new creation in Christ Jesus—and armed with a new commission: to destroy the works of the devil and expose him, so that many souls could be set free.

CHAPTER
ONE

The Cunning Serpent

The greatest trick the devil ever pulled was to convince the world he didn't exist.[1]

The first thing you need to know about the spiritual being called Satan, or the devil, is that you won't find him running around in a red suit, with horns and a pitchfork. He won't come at you with bared fangs dripping blood. No! He would much rather you fall for the lie that he is just a myth and he doesn't exist at all. But if he can't convince you to swallow that, his next move will be to invade your life with all the hidden powers of hell, unseen but deadly.

When Jesus walked the earth, He warned us that the devil has a three-pronged mission: to kill, steal, and destroy.

But then He added these precious words: "I have come that they may have life, and that they may have it more abundantly." Yes, the devil is real and very powerful, but there is someone more powerful than he: Jesus, the Son of God. If you don't know Him yet, my prayer is that by the end of this book you will.

In these pages I want to share with you how to uncover all the different ways the devil tries to invade your life. I will peel back the mask he's hiding behind and disclose his true nature, so you can be armed and ready when he comes. Together we will explore the reality of spiritual warfare and what it means to be a true soldier of the Cross. That's military language for good reason: you and I are in a war, an unseen spiritual war that reaches all around us, all the time. This is a war of darkness versus light, good versus evil. I should know; for twenty-five years I fought on the side of darkness, climbing the ranks of Santeria, Palo Mayombe, and spiritualism until I was the devil's number 3 man in New York City, casting spells and plunging whole neighborhoods into Satan's grip. You can read my testimony in the book *Out of the Devil's Cauldron*.

Big Dreams, Little People

I want to take you back for a moment to your younger years and mine. I remember in my first grade class one spring afternoon in early May, my teacher sat us down in a circle and asked us the ultimate question: "What do you want to be when you grow up?"

As I looked around the room in a panic, my heart racing a hundred miles an hour, I felt excited but afraid at the same time. Glancing around the classroom in a daze, with the big bright windows and bright yellow-painted walls, what stood out to me that moment was our finest artwork, displayed beautifully on the wall. Some of the artwork had little green hands, while others featured drawings of family faces or a few stick-figure family portraits.

As the teacher asked us this question, one by one, our emotions ran high. The excitement in the room was so thick you could almost cut it, as little people with big dreams yelled out "Me first; me first!" In the background I could hear some of my classmates yelling at the top of their lungs: "I want to be a police officer!" "I want to be an astronaut!" or "I want to be a fireman!" On the other side of the room another one yelled out, "I want to be a doctor!" Other classmates, their faces showing their confusion, didn't know what to say. Most of the girls agreed on being a nurse or a schoolteacher—or maybe even a ballerina. Surely, that was a fun day in class.

Nothing in our young hearts and minds was hoping and believing to become anything evil. Not even for a second , or a moment in time, did anyone yell out, "I want to be a murderer! I can't wait to grow up and be a serial killer or a drug dealer." Nor did any of the girls in the class raise their hands and say, "I want to be a prostitute and sell my body for money, or be in a bad relationship and later on get murdered." None of us that day had shattered dreams or false hopes.

As an ex-devil worshiper, I believe that the day you are born you start to die. You haven't yet said your first words, you haven't taken your first step, but as soon as you breathe your first breath, the devil has assigned a demon to chase after your life.

The thief comes only to steal and kill and destroy; I have come that they may have life, and have it to the full (John 10:10 NIV).

From the first breath you take, the devil and his demons' plans are to keep you away from the truth of knowing where you came from, away from knowing that you were designed to have a relationship with your creator, Jesus Christ, and away from knowing that at the end of the journey you are to return to where you came from: eternity with God. The plan of the enemy, whether you live in the penthouse or in the ghetto, is to distract every step of your life that was predestined by God to get you back home with Him. There was a discussion in Heaven before He gave you a birth date and sent you into time. "Before I formed you in the womb I knew you, before you were born I set you apart; I appointed you as a prophet to the nations" (Jer. 1:5 NIV).

The Mind—Satan's Battlefield

Let me bring you into the enemy's kingdom and the strategy of the devil in a deeper way. The first thing the enemy attacks is your mind.

The enemy knows that the battle is in the mind, and he knows if he can capture the territory of your mind, your thoughts, and the way you operate, he's got you in a stranglehold. The next move he makes will be to attack your soul. This includes your mind, will, and emotions. Once he's got a person's soul, he will paralyze that person and bring them down to nothing. He has done this for centuries. He did it with Adam and Eve and with their son Cain, who murdered his brother, Abel. He did it with King Saul, who committed suicide, and with Judas Iscariot, who sold Jesus for thirty pieces of silver and later committed suicide.

And so, dear brothers and sisters, I plead with you to give your bodies [and minds] *to God because of all He has done for you. Let them be a living and holy sacrifice—the kind He will find acceptable. This is truly the way to worship Him. Don't copy the behavior and customs of this world, but let God transform you into a new person by changing the way you think. Then you will learn to know God's will for you, which is good and pleasing and perfect* (Rom. 12:1-2 NLT).

Doing this will keep you in the perfect will of God and out of the hands of the enemy, who wants to destroy your life. I believe that many Christians read the Word but never act on it, and the danger of this is that we leave ourselves open, unguarded, to the enemy's devices and entrapments and to the strongholds of the Satanic world. If we want to be more than conquerors, reading the Word is not enough. Acting on the Word and applying it—mixing it with faith—will destroy the enemy's game plan for your life.

The devil and his principalities (high-ranking evil spirits), who run the first and second heavens, and the junior "ground-level" demons, who operate on the earth today, have one mission—to capture your mind in a way that brings you to the point of no return. The enemy is clever; he studies each person—their character, their personality, their bad habits, their strong points and weaknesses. Then he sets traps based on all the information he has gathered, whether that person is a believer in Christ Jesus or not. He knows how to wait for the right opportunity to open the spirit realm in your life. This is how he gets that entry point into your life.

Baby Steps Toward Destruction

For example, people like Charles Manson, Jeffrey Dahmer, Ted Bundy, and those who initiate mass shootings, and the beheadings in the Middle East all have one thing in common: they hear voices in their heads. The enemy has stolen their characters, their personalities, their will, and emotions because he was able to break them down to nothing and strip them of their identity. When I was a general in the devil's kingdom myself, I was taught these tactics of how to strip a person down to nothing and steal their identity.

The enemy knows how to set you up to take baby steps into the progression of your destruction. One of the most incredible psalms is Psalm 91. Look at what verses 3 and 13 say:

> *Surely He shall deliver thee from the snare of the fowler, and from the noisome pestilence. Thou shalt tread upon the lion and adder: the young lion and the dragon shalt thou trample under feet* (Ps. 91:3,13).

In these two Scriptures, the fowler represents the devil. I want to pinpoint his entrapments, which are the lion, the adder, the young lion, and the dragon. These are tools the enemy uses to set you up. The one that is most dangerous of all is the young lion. It is the setup that you don't see coming. This entrapment is smooth, under the radar, and it is the one opportunity described that you give the enemy to use against you. The young lion represents a "small" sin that you think you can control and put away whenever you want. For example, it could be watching porn movies or listening to dirty lyrics on a CD; it could be watching pornography on the Internet. It could also be smoking a marijuana cigarette once in a while.

Another example could be going to places that you know you shouldn't go as a believer. Let me give you the strongest warning someone could ever give you in your life. *When you play around with or entertain a "young lion," what you don't end up killing and putting away from you now will end up killing you: because when it's full-grown it becomes the lion or dragon that Psalm 91:13 describes.* That's how the enemy gets his way to build strongholds in your life.

Common Gateways and Portals

Here are some other gateways and portals the enemy uses to keep you away from God's best. Many of the things listed below are activities people engage in (even as children or teenagers) thinking they are just "innocent fun." I'm here to tell you, there's nothing innocent about them. Take part in any of the following and you are playing with fire—and propping the door wide open for the enemy's activity in your life:

- Mediums, psychics, fortune-tellers
- Tarot card readings
- Séances
- Horoscopes
- Paranormal phenomena
- Talking to the dead
- Seeking after ghosts
- Playing with Ouija boards
- Watching horror movies or television shows

- Listening to music with lyrics of profanity, murder, suicide, etc.

- Pornography

These are the devil's weapons of mass destruction that he uses against humanity without them even knowing it. Satan has a PhD in capturing your imagination. Once he has a hold of that, he then takes control of your life and owns it. In his timing, he will take your life out. He starts with your imagination and won't stop there. It will become a ripple effect into your family. Have you ever heard someone say, "My daddy was an alcoholic, and his daddy was too" or "So many people in my family tree committed suicide"? Why do you think there are so many generational curses, so much sickness, and so much destruction within families? That was never God's intent for our lives.

My warning as a watchman on the wall is this: stay away from these things!

The Devil Doesn't Discriminate

The devil doesn't work only in our normal lives or environment; he's after every piece of territory he can get. The devil's plan is that if he can take over the territory, he can control the people. He's out to claim territory, or spiritual regions, regardless of status—rich or poor, black or white, famous or obscure. I'll give you one example of this.

The devil goes to Hollywood. We watch television celebrities and movie stars and think they are sitting on top of the world. Some of us want to be them; we envy them; we even go so far as to imitate them and look like them. But if people in Hollywood could testify and speak the truth from their hearts, many of them would give anything to switch places with us. If you look deeply into Hollywood, you can see the face of the devil and how he has so many people in his pocket for a season.

These people shine like stars, but look again—the stars are falling. They suffer from depression, oppression, suicide, out-of-control lust, diseases, alcoholism, drug addiction; many are on so many prescription pills they can't keep track of them anymore. From famous singers to stars of the big screen and small screen (television), somehow, somewhere, they have made a pact with the devil. Some of the most famous Latino singers, for example, have reached the heights of success only to end up in a coffin, to be buried in a cemetery in the Bronx. If I were to name the name of one particular singer, you would know her songs. She sold her life to the occult "religion" called Santeria. Many others today are on the same route, on a train called "Hellbound," and the motorman also has a name: his name is the devil. So the stars in Hollywood are falling.

The Devil Knows Your Neighborhood

Don't let these words scare you, but it's true: the enemy knows your neighborhood—and I don't mean in a Sesame Street type of way! Do you know your neighborhood as a believer in Christ? Demons are assigned to patrol and control your neighborhood: principalities, and junior demons taking orders from them. I want to give you a glimpse into the unseen demonic world. As an ex-demonic evangelist, I know the ins and outs of that world, how Satan strategically plants strongholds in our neighborhoods, and every day we walk by the strongholds and they become the norm to us.

Let me name a few of those strongholds in your neighborhood:

Mosques

A demonic place where the devil meets with his people, yet we pass by it every day and brush it off like it's nothing instead of laying hands on it, cursing it to the root, and removing it. These demonic temples are right in our territory where our families live and our children play.

Many people think Islam is an innocent religion. It is not. We are easily fooled because we see Muslims living their morals and staying faithful to the core of their religion, but what most people don't realize is that the "god" of Islam is a demon called Allah. These individuals are like sleeper agents until they are pressed to the point to defend their religion; then they manifest, and turn on you and on society.

At the carwash where I get my car serviced, 95 percent of the workers are Muslim. They are very kind and seem to be very genuine, but as soon as I start talking about Jesus Christ as the Son of God, or about radical Islam or the stuff on the news today, or how if a person leaves Islam they have a death sentence on their life and it shouldn't be that way—you should see their reaction. From acting nice and genuine, their features change and their body language changes and they start to manifest to another person.

Botanicas

The *botanica* is another place, another stronghold where people go to get tarot card readings and buy candles to do witchcraft with. Many people think that botanicas are just a part of the Spanish culture—no harm, no foul. They couldn't be more mistaken. These shops sell ingredients for the purposes of black magic. And when people get tarot card readings to make contact with dead relatives, what they don't realize is that the "relative" who shows up is a familiar spirit, a demon that mimics everything about the deceased person.

Liquor Stores

Liquor stores in our neighborhoods are breaking families up through a spirit of alcoholism. This spirit is destroying families, loved ones, friends, and entire neighborhoods, and we do nothing about it. When was the last time we prayed and took inventory of our own neighborhood and claimed it for Jesus Christ and believed God to turn it around?

Nightclubs

Whether they are Latin nightclubs playing Spanish music, or R&B, or rap music, or rock clubs, or techno clubs, it's all the devil's playground. The neighborhoods they are located in are under the control of spirits of lust, immorality, adultery, alcoholism, drugs, murder—the list is long. You may think you can go out for a night of dancing and innocent fun. Think again. When you head back home, those demons follow you to infiltrate your whole environment.

I believe the reason we are put in our neighborhood is to destroy the works of the devil. For that reason and that reason alone, God has given you a place to reside in that particular neighborhood. Many neighborhoods are under a curse of control by demonic forces, by spirits of murder, suicide, poverty, immorality, adultery, and homosexuality, by spirits of insanity that know how to steal your mind, spirits assigned to break up families, spirits of rape, molestation, and so on.

This warning goes out to Christians today. Many of us take it upon ourselves to move on our own understanding, either to another state, city, region, or borough (this can be like committing spiritual suicide). We so easily allow the enemy to relocate us. It doesn't matter if it's a high-end neighborhood or a low-income neighborhood; demons are assigned everywhere. We easily fall into the trap—the trap of the hands of the devil—and become victims instead of being victorious in Christ. We don't pray and seek the heart of God. We don't fast anymore. We don't even inquire if it's God's perfect will for us to move geographically, when the devil may be setting us up to fall into his pit of destruction.

This does not only affect you, it affects your family too, chipping away at their purpose and destiny. You need to come to see that your purpose and destiny are also lined up with the region and the season you are in.

The number one danger for a Christian is to move out of God's timing. It is like trying to clap with one hand. Beware of the enemy's plan for your life. God has a plan and purpose for your life, but so does the enemy. "Lest Satan should get an advantage of us: for we are not ignorant of his devices" (2 Cor. 2:11).

It's so important for us to pray and hear from God before we make any moves, anywhere. The devil is looking for an opportunity to set us up. He knows the dangers of moving out of God's timing. He will seduce you with a better place, better school, and better opportunities. But remember: Just because something shines and looks good to us doesn't mean that God is in it. So be careful.

Pray before you take your next step. The devil knows how to place you in a neighborhood that you're not prepared for spiritually. The plan he is trying to accomplish is to dismantle you spiritually by placing you in one of his stronghold places, or a neighborhood that he controls. He does this to dismantle you and your family, to destroy or delay the plan that God has for your life.

One of the craziest things I've heard since being a Christian, and the thing that breaks my heart, is what comes out of the mouths of my brothers and sisters in the Lord when they're trying to move to another city or country. They say, "I wonder if there are any good schools there?" or "Are there any good shopping areas, or buses and trains close by?" I've never heard a Christian say, "I wonder if there's a Bible-believing church in the area that preaches the Word of God uncompromised." They are not concerned about their purpose or destiny in God, or the consequences of eternity. That's when you know the devil is setting you up.

Who Is Seducing You?

I believe every person has two doors in their lives. One of the doors is your mind and the other is your heart. These areas are "gateways" into your soul. God and the devil are in a battle for the doors of your life.

"Behold, I stand at the door, and knock: if any man hear my voice, and open the door, I will come in to him, and will sup with him, and he with me" (Rev. 3:20). Who owns the doors in your life? Ask yourself this question, and be honest. I am offering you a "Get Out of Hell Free" card. I am asking you with an honest heart to reflect on this question: where do you want to spend eternity? I want to silence the voice of reasoning in your life. Sad to say, in many churches today, instead of listening to the voice of the Holy Spirit, people are captured and held hostage by the voice of their reasoning, which is the voice of the devil himself. He holds our minds and thoughts captive in such a way that brings circumstances and consequences to our Christian walk. This makes it difficult to "fight the good fight of faith" as believers in the Lord Jesus Christ.

When God gives us a test and we are taking the class, many Christians today, instead of getting an "A" and passing the test, end up with an "Incomplete" in life. It's like going to college and taking an expensive course, and somewhere in the middle we opt out and settle for an "Incomplete." A life that's lived in alignment with the Scriptures—a life of sold-out obedience to the Lord Jesus Christ—is the greatest defense against the evil one. Don't settle for an incomplete. Determine in your heart to go all the way with God, "being confident of this, that He who began a good work in you will carry it on to completion until the day of Christ Jesus" (Phil. 1:6 NIV).

In Chapter 3 we'll look at some more examples of these open doors in your life, which the apostle Paul called the fiery darts of the devil and his cronies. These are the entrapments they use to try to succeed over your life. But first I want to talk about his number one setup—that's the subject of the next Chapter.

Summary

The craftiness of the devil has trapped fallen humanity—and all of modern society—in a gross lie. So many people are tied up in the hands of this creature called the devil, and they don't even realize it. From our earliest childhood to the end of our lives, if someone doesn't sound the trumpet and point to the Cross of Jesus Christ, we are doomed.

Note

1. A line made famous by the movie *The Usual Suspects* (Polygram Filmed Entertainment, 1995).

> *The greatest trick the devil ever pulled was*
> *to convince the world he didn't exist.*

Identity Theft—the Devil's Favorite Game

Adam and Eve were created perfect by God, and the devil stole their identity. In the same way, the devil steals many believers' and unbelievers' identities by robbing and stripping them of who God created them to be.

The devil's ultimate purpose in his kingdom, with his demons and principalities, is to steal your identity. This tactic is designed to keep a person from the Cross, redemption, and salvation. It progresses from taking their purpose and identity to leaving that person just barely surviving.

Listen to these beautiful words of God to each of us:

Before I formed you in the womb I knew you; before you were born I sanctified you; I ordained you a prophet to the nations (Jer. 1:5 NKJV).

"Before I formed you, I knew you"—that means that in eternity past you had a meeting with God. One of the reasons He was going to send you down to creation, through a birthday, through a place in time, was to fulfill an assignment. Yet somewhere in a hospital room (or wherever you were birthed), the devil assigned a demon to your life, to steal your identity.

Today we hear a lot about identity theft, which is when someone steals your social security number, your credit cards, and your bank accounts; we know that situation is a living hell. It can take months or even years to recover from the damages. Now imagine someone stealing your identity *spiritually*. This type of damage intertwines with your eternity and determines where you will end up. The devil has been doing this since the beginning of time.

Throughout the Bible we read of the lives of men like King Saul, Samson, Esau, Jonathan, and Judas; these are some of the names of people who allowed the enemy to get the best of them. If we were to discuss the names of people today whose lives the enemy has hijacked—people whose spiritual identities have been stolen—there would be millions of names.

The devil is trying his best to steal our identity and the identity of the Church itself. Following are some of the ways he operates, or tries to operate, in our lives, to take our identity.

Marriages and Families

In my past life as a devil worshiper, I was taught and trained to have no mercy in attacking the family through witchcraft to

34

break their unity and separate them from one another, especially if they were married.

The devil hates human beings because we are made in the image of God; that's the one thing he hates most. The second thing he hates is the family. Those who work for his kingdom through witchcraft, the occult, and spiritualism (such as casting spells) are trained to destroy families because the family represents Christ in the Church. If you dismantle the family, you strip it from its true identity.

Let me share something very important here. The devil is OK with so-called families, or people who are involved in homosexuality: Men living with men and women living with women. When it was time to do witchcraft on them, we didn't have to dismantle the family at all because they were already in sin. To teach them a lesson when they crossed the line against us, we would attack their bodies with a spirit of infirmity so they would die; because their identity was already stolen.

Workplace

Another place demons will attack to destroy and bring chaos to your life is through your workplace. If you are the man of the house—or the head of the home, as Christians call it—your identity is wrapped up in your ability to provide for your family. Wreaking havoc in this area will break and dismantle your finances, and divide and steal your home. The devil also frequently uses the workplace as a place of temptation to adultery and fornication, encouraging two people to form a "friendship" that escalates into full-blown immorality.

Health

The devil will also seek after your health through addictions, drugs, alcohol, diseases, and sickness because he knows that your body was created to be the temple of the Holy Spirit (whether you're a believer or not). This is another way that he's an identity thief.

Finances

Your money is another area the devil will attack. Out-of-control finances will push you to create such a debt factor in your life that it often brings oppression, depression, anger, resentment, and even spirits of suicide into your life. As we know, many today couldn't carry that weight, and it has taken the lives of young and old, male and female, from all walks of life.

Relationships

Through abusive relationships, the devil steals your identity and your self-confidence. He releases a spirit of condemnation on you, a spirit of low self-esteem, and allows a spirit of torment to scorn your mind—to the point that you think nothing is left of yourself. He also uses improper relationships to introduce you to spirits of adultery and fornication, wrapping you so tight in a web of immorality that only the power of the Holy Spirit can break it.

These are many of the gateways that this monster called the devil uses to steal your identity. I have no respect for him whatsoever. He will take every opportunity to devour and eat away at your true identity.

Be sober, be vigilant; because your adversary the devil, as a roaring lion, walketh about, seeking whom he may devour: whom resist stedfast in the faith, knowing that the same afflictions are accomplished in your brethren that are in the world (1 Pet. 5:8-9).

I want to leave you with a thought. I heard this from a great preacher once. Please examine yourself on the basis of what I am about to share with you. If you have a dozen eggs and two break, how many are left? Would you then throw away the whole carton? The same is true of your life. Why would you quit and throw in the towel? Why would you turn away from God, and, if you're not a believer, why wouldn't you give God a chance? The point I am trying to convey to you is this: just because two circumstances of your life are not going the way you wanted, but ten circumstances are still good and healthy, why would you want to give up or give in to the enemy and throw your life away?

Temptation and Deception: Twin Evils

The tools that the devil uses most often are temptation and deception. Temptation is to make you want to quit and give up on God, and deception is to make you believe that you're never going to come out of your circumstances. Satan has been plaguing the Church of Jesus Christ with these two lies since the beginning of time. But I encourage you, believer, not to fall into these traps. Examine yourself when the enemy is trying to afflict you with these two lies. Know that God is faithful, and look behind your shoulder, whether you've been saved one year, ten years, or twenty years; look at the footprints of Jesus behind you that have brought you up to this point, and see that God has never failed you. Hold on to that picture in your heart and mind through faith, and then you will not fall into the entrapments of this loser called the Adversary.

One of the greatest things the enemy does is to cause a person to make a permanent decision based on a temporary situation. I believe we get stuck on the broken parts of our lives and sit in those areas far too long, even though we know that storms don't last. It's time to get up from the ashes and dust ourselves off from the residue of life, look the enemy eye to eye, and take back our identity. In case you've lost it and can't find it, your identity starts at the Cross. Get back to that place, where everything begins and ends in Jesus Christ.

> *Therefore, if anyone is in Christ, he is a new creation; the old has gone, the new is here!* (2 Cor. 5:17 NIV)

Summary

How easy we make it for the devil to steal our identity. We are all born with a purpose for our lives from the hands of God—but then the fiery darts of temptation and deception invade our lives. I call them spiritual bombs, entrapments of the enemy, setups that take our very lives in a downward spiral from God's best, which He designed for us before the beginning of time.

CHAPTER
THREE

Shutting Open Doors

One of the biggest deceptions the enemy uses on believers today, and how he opens doors in their lives, is to convince them that they have their sin situation under control and can quit at any given time. This is the number one setup the devil uses to create strongholds in the life of a Christian.

Sometimes he hooks them into watching Internet pornography by placing little drops of temptation in their mind, or inflames an urge to discover pornographic movies. Sometimes he flashes images in the mind to captivate and seduce the person to their computer so they can fall into that trap. He plays on their emotions to open a gateway of the mind to have their body react a certain way that will leave the person with a sexual temptation to perform unnatural acts against their own body—acts that are against the will of God.

I have encountered Christians who have fallen into the filthy hands of the devil in these situations, and their minds have become so diluted that they confessed that performing pleasurable acts against their own body is not a sin. That is a lie from the pit of hell!

Falling for the Lie

The enemy will open portals, or doorways, to bring someone back to their past in their mind, before they were saved, especially if the person was delivered from certain strongholds such as drinking, drug addiction, or fornication, for example. He will use those old strongholds to tempt that person in order to bring them back to that place over and over. In a subtle, convincing way, the enemy will try to convince you that the grace of God will cover you and that it's OK to give into those temptations He has delivered you from. This is called *premeditated sin*. The grace of God should never be taken for granted.

In a similar way, if there was a season in our past in which we struggled with things such as unbelief, self-condemnation, shamefulness, abuse, or rejection, the demons will find ways—through our church, through other believers, or especially through family members—to bring us back to the ashes of these circumstances that the Lord has delivered or healed us from.

Another weapon that the enemy knows how to use is the negative words that come out of other people's mouths or—even worse—out of our own, to set up the trap that will drag us back into the mud. Our Christian walk shouldn't be that way. "The tongue has the power of life and death, and those who love it will eat its fruit" (Proverbs 18:21 NIV).

Happy Words vs. True Freedom

Many of the churches today (thank God not all) are "preaching us happy" but are never freeing us from the attacks of the enemy, from the pitfalls of life, and from the entrapments of the devil. These churches are not freeing us from broken marriages, from backsliders in our families, from bad soul ties, from generational curses that are never dealt with but are swept under the carpet, because the Church is not discipling us to receive the true freedom we have in the authority of Jesus Christ.

I have heard many times over from brothers and sisters in the Lord that they are led by the hand of demons into situations without realizing they are being set up. All you hear from these precious brothers and sisters is "I have a check in my spirit about that person," but they are not able to discern the danger that is ahead. Many times the devil sends people our way to destroy our destiny when God warns us to stay away.

Destiny Stealers

If we are caught unawares, we may miss God's warnings and fall into the enemy's hands and so create bad soul ties and bondages in our life. There is also another danger we seldom speak about that the enemy uses against us—it's the setup of being unequally yoked with unbelievers, or even marrying the wrong believer. Many times people have married another Christian that the Lord has not hand-selected for them: maybe because that person is not spiritually mature, or maybe there are things they haven't surrendered to the Lord, or maybe they are not connected spiritually to the ministry God has called you for. They could also be a wolf in sheep's clothing, handpicked by the enemy to sabotage your ministry or your life.

The Bible is filled with stories we can learn from, about how to stay free from bondages and shackles that lead to bad soul ties. One of the saddest examples in the Old Testament has to do with Jonathan and King Saul, his father. When God gave this young man Jonathan a good soul tie, who was David, instead of cultivating that good soul tie, he kept his alliance and commitment to his dad. Jonathan felt obligated to go with his father all the way. I can only imagine if Jonathan had done a 180-degree turn and followed David. What would his life have been like? But because of that one bad soul tie, he came to an early death.

How can many Christians learn from this, including myself? These are strong warnings that we should never take lightly. The Lord has allowed these warnings to be in His Word for our own protection against the enemy. The devil knows our carnal desires better than we know ourselves. Many times he takes advantage when we give him those opportunities to create bad soul ties.

I say this with a sad heart, but many Christians today, because of the lust of the eyes and flesh and the pride of life, have made some bad decisions instead of agreeing with God. They came into agreement with the devil, and because of the consequences of their choices, they are not living God's best for their lives.

A Divine Partnership

Do you know that you are in partnership with God? Do you know that there is a covenant made within this partnership? When you accepted Jesus in your life, you made an agreement to be in a partnership and you made a commitment to keep your end of the deal, to fight the good fight of faith (see 1 Tim. 6:12 and 2 Tim. 4:7).

The enemy is looking for every opportunity to distort, delay, and even to void your part of the contract. Many of my brothers and sisters today start strong, but somewhere down the line the demons get a hold of them and sabotage their part of their contract. Many have backslidden, and even have the audacity to say that Jesus didn't work for them. Truth be told, though, they never kept their end of the deal; Jesus works all the time, and all things work together for good for those who love Him.

Warning: who have you tied yourself to: the Cross or the world? The Bible says, "Don't team up with those who are unbelievers. How can righteousness be a partner with wickedness? How can light live with darkness?" (2 Cor. 6:14 NLT)

Let me leave you with this thought: Do you know the voice of God for your life? Or have you been listening to the voice of the devil?

Summary

How easily we as believers, and especially nonbelievers, allow the devil and his henchmen to open doors in our lives, quick as lightning, but it takes a lifetime for us to close them. Be watchful in your walk with God. The devil is after us nonstop.

Many of us are so quick to believe the enemy of our lives over the eternal God, Jesus Christ, who created us—falling hard to the words we speak that are lifeless, that are hurting ourselves, hurting others, and grieving the heart of God.

If we are not vigilant, we may let our life slip away through the pitfalls of delay, believing distorted truth, generational curses, demonic friendships, and the people we connect to (bad soul ties), and so wind up missing God's best. The devil is relentless, but we have the victory in Jesus Christ. It's time to close those doors and never look back. Trust in the finished work of the Cross.

CHAPTER
FOUR

The Voice of God and the Voice of the Devil

There are two roads in life, two directions, two voices, two paths, but only one journey, with signs and warnings ahead of us. If you had the opportunity to ponder your life today and look back and reflect on where you are standing, which highway of life would you enter and what signs were ahead? Which exits did you miss where you were supposed to get off? I believe that if you look hard enough into your journey, you will know that there are two voices trying to direct your path: the voice of God and the voice of the devil. Look at how different these two voices are.

GOD	DEVIL
Stills you	Torments you
Reassures you	Threatens you
Leads you	Pushes you
Enlightens you	Confuses you
Forgives you	Condemns you
Calms you	Stresses you
Encourages you	Discourages you
Comforts you	Worries you

The thief does not come except to steal, and to kill, and to destroy. I have come that they may have life, and that they may have it more abundantly (John 10:10 NKJV).

One voice leads to victory regardless of the potholes you encounter on the highways of life. Another voice comes to delay, steal, and alter the plans and purposes of your destiny and how it's supposed to play out in your lifetime. That other voice brings torment, sickness, confusion, fear, doubt, unbelief, letdowns, entrapments, delays, chaos, oppression, depression, suicide, even sometimes murder in the journey called life. That voice will steal your life away, regardless of who you are. It will give you the worst deck of cards that you could ever imagine and put you on the road to spiritual death, to the point of no return.

Caution: The Bible tells us that Satan can appear as an angel of light, and increasingly I see him using tactics to mimic the true Light—Jesus Christ—through New Age practices. Many times, people will fall into the trap of speaking to their "inner guide" or "spirit guide" or "ascended self." This garbage goes by a lot of different names, but the reality is that they're entertaining familiar spirits: Spirits who speak loving, self-affirming words to them and teach them "higher knowledge." My point is that you may hear sweet words and think, *this has to be God,"* because the devil likes to mimic everything God does, but with a perverted twist.

If a person continues on this path, the end result will be ugly. Eventually those spirits' true colors will show up, and the person's bondage will be complete. Anyone who practices "channeling" of spirit guides needs serious deliverance—a subject we'll get into later in this book. This is a form of witchcraft and demonic possession.

Don't be fooled, people. Ask God to help you discern good from evil. Holy angels do not have ongoing conversations with people; they may appear from time to time to deliver a message or encouraging word (we see this in the Bible), but if any "angel" tells you it's from God and wants to have a "walking/talking/guiding" relationship with you—it's a demonic spirit, pure and simple.

Two Voices in a Garden

Let me take you back to the place where it all began—the voice of God comforted Adam and Eve in the Garden of Eden, where they had His sweet fellowship in their lives, day after day. But an interruption took place in the midst of the Garden, a second voice that was pure poison, and that voice came from the serpent, the devil himself, lying through his teeth. Here's a recap of the encounter that took place in the Garden of Eden:

> *But the serpent said to the woman, "You will not surely die. For God knows that when you eat of it your eyes will be opened, and you will be like God, knowing good and evil"* (Gen. 3:4-5 ESV).

Prior to this conversation, God gave an order of trust, and told Adam and Eve that they could eat from any tree in the Garden except the Tree of the Knowledge of Good and Evil. I believe the reason God allowed this, and gave this order, was to give them freedom of will and build trust between God and man—which brings us into a pure relationship with God, based on those principles.

So here Adam and Eve had two trees, or really two opportunities to choose right from wrong; because if they disobeyed God's one command, He said they would surely die, which refers to spiritual death—and eventually results in physical death.

The devil, in his craftiness, seized the opportunity to turn man against God. How did he do this? By trickery of speech and by twisting God's words. That caused the Fall of man, and this has affected us down through the generations; until now, we think we have become like God, making our own decisions. Not only has the Fall decayed our lives and our families, but this entire world, by causing us to play God.

But in God's mercy, He spared Adam and Eve, by killing an animal in their place. This showed that someone innocent had to die on their behalf, which is a foreshadowing of the coming of the Messiah, Jesus Christ. Sin came into the world through Adam's sinful choice, but redemption was coming right after it.

God already had a plan of salvation in motion. And today, as rebellious people, we have rejected that gift of redemption, and the devil laughs and is still conquering the opportunity for us to not only play God, but to keep spiritual death in humanity. Doors are also opened to demonic activity in the lives of those who reject God's way of salvation.

This is how spiritual warfare was born. God has given the Church the victory against the enemy and his kingdom. It's up to us to reinforce that victory.

Which Voice Will You Choose?

Since that day in the Garden, down through the generations, many people have harkened to that voice of Satan. We have played a game to be God, thinking that we can be our own God, knowing right from wrong or good from evil. We have come down to nothing, a life of bad decisions, a life of emptiness and sorrow, but we don't have to stay there. I come to bring you good news; there is another voice—the one true Voice—and His name is King Jesus. He is the only way out from any nightmare you are facing today. It's time to turn to the Cross of Jesus Christ. Life is too short. "Whereas you do not know what will happen tomorrow. For what is your life? It is even a vapor that appears for a little time and then vanishes away" (James 4:14 NKJV).

Take a moment to examine yourself. You only have one life to live. If you knew you had only five years, ten years, twenty years, or even just days left of your life, what decisions would you make? Would you allow the devil to steal your life away? If you had one trip to make to the Post Office of Eternity and you asked the clerk for a change of address form, which address would you put on the form? Would it be Heaven or hell? Let's not even mention purgatory, as it doesn't exist.

In the Gospel of John during the crucifixion, there were two thieves on the cross; one repented and Jesus said to him, "Today you will be with Me in Paradise," which means Heaven, not purgatory. The other thief harkened to the wrong voice, and his outcome wasn't a pretty one, as he ended up in hell.

I leave you with this thought. I, John Ramirez, was given a second chance after twenty-five years of devil worshiping. If you are reading this chapter, this is your second chance. The God I know is a God of mercy, a God of grace, and a God of love.

This is your second chance. So please fill out this form and choose the way to your new home for eternity.

CHANGE OF ADDRESS FORM:

First Name:_____ Last Name:_____

Current Address: _____

Earth—Funeral Home of Your Choice: _____

Final Destination: Heaven or Hell? _____

Heaven is a place of peace, joy, love, mansions that go for miles, a place of no sickness or disease, no hurt, no torment, no pain, no tears, worship as you never heard on earth—a place where we won't ever say goodbye because no one ever dies, and the greatest joy is to be with Jesus.

Hell, which was created for the devil and his demons, is a place where you never see your loved ones again. It is a place of lowliness, torment, rejection, and despair—a place where your thoughts will remind you of how many times you rejected the free gift of salvation. In hell, souls are ripped apart by the tormentors, sorrow reigns forever, the smell of death (sulfur) pervades the atmosphere, and the only song you will ever hear is the wailing and screams of those who are there forever. There is no hope of ever escaping hell, because of the decisions that got you there.

> *For God so loved the world that He gave His only begotten Son, that whoever believes in Him should not perish but have everlasting life* (John 3:16 NKJV).

Practical Spiritual Counsel for the Believer Today

Let's put hell on notice and be the victorious Christians that God called us to be. I want to educate believers and teach them how to stay free and out of the grips of the enemy. I would love to help many of my brothers and sisters who are not aware of spiritual warfare prayers. They depend on general prayers in their life to defeat the onslaught and the weapons of mass destruction that the devil has unleashed against the Church of Jesus Christ. General prayers don't work. The devil doesn't mind that we pray general prayers against the hellacious personal attacks in our lives. As a matter of fact, he loves it because they are ineffective.

Before we dive deeper into spiritual warfare in the upcoming chapters, let's go over a few things so you have a strategy for defeating the devil.

Step 1—Don't Fear: The first thing believers should do when under attack is fear not. Don't panic and don't let the devil put pressure on you in any attack or spiritual circumstance. As I mentioned in Chapter Two, one of the cleverest tactics the enemy uses is to get us to make a *permanent decision based on a temporary situation*. That clever deception costs us spiritual setbacks and delays in hearing from God. Always remember: storms don't last. The Word of the Lord says to be still and know that He is God (see Ps. 46:10).

For example, let's say the devil attacks you in the church you're going to. Somebody snubs you when you walk in the door, or a group of gossips starts talking about you. You get upset and angry, decide to take it personally, and leave the church. Rather than praying and seeking God for your best answer, you let the devil push you out of the church that God positioned you in for your spiritual growth. Now you run out from there to another church, spiritually disjointed because you made a decision in the flesh, and the devil uprooted you from the position of God's perfect will for you in that season and that place. You just made a permanent decision based on a temporary situation; now the devil's got you.

Step 2—Do Periodic Checkups: To avoid the gradual slide into sin and selfishness that plagues unwary believers, I recommend that you make an assessment every three months of where you are spiritually. Make an assessment of your relationship with Jesus and the season you find yourself in.

Trial, Test, ...or Open Door?

One of the things we should ask ourselves when the devil releases his demonic agents against us is the following question: "Is this a trial or a test, or did I open a door to the enemy?" When we open doors to the enemy, we give the devil legal rights over that part of our life, creating strongholds that need to be broken.

Let me explain these steps further. A *trial* is a situation or circumstance that lasts for a long period of time, such as we read about in the book of Job. Historians say that Job's trial lasted a year. A trial could be many things, such as a financial setback, a marriage struggle, an illness or infirmity—such as when I went blind again in 2002, for no reason at all; it was an attack from the devil. That's when we have to make a decision: Either we trust God through the trial or we collapse.

A *test* is something that has a shorter season of attack, something we can go through in days or weeks, depending on how we handle ourselves in the battle. A test could be a bad day at work, or a weeklong series of bad situations, or small circumstances that frustrate, anger, or depress you. An example of a test would be falling out at work with a co-worker, or perhaps an unsaved family member offends you. How you react can either glorify God or open doors to the enemy. You know that you have passed the test when you either humble yourself and accept the situation, or you turn away from it and leave with peace in your heart, knowing you did what God expected you to do.

An *open door* is when we step out of the will of God and so give the devil a legal right to have the upper hand over us.

It is important to identify which of these you are confronting, so you can prepare for battle and trust God for your victory. If you're not sure, ask the Lord to reveal the answer to you, but usually there are distinguishing characteristics to each.

The snares of the devil could be watching unholy television shows and movies, because the devil is the prince of the air (he controls the media and has domains over it); what you speak out of your mouth, because the devil is after your words; or any gossip you entertain that comes in through your ears that contaminates your spirit man. Another very common open door that many Christians allow is being ensnared by the filth of pornography. The Bible makes it clear that you must guard your eye gate, ear gate, and mouth gate because these are portals that give the enemy legal rights to create strongholds in your life and entrapments that will damage your walk in the Light with the Lord Jesus Christ.

One of the things the devil doesn't want the believer to know is that the victory was already won at the Cross of Jesus Christ. All we have to do is reinforce that victory. It is sad to say that many of us, because we get caught up in looking at the circumstances of the battle in the natural, lose focus on that victory Jesus Christ has already won. We serve a supernatural God.

Summary

You have a choice in this life—serve God or follow the devil. Two voices, two paths, but only one choice. I know it often doesn't seem that black and white, but it is. If we are not moving forward with God, taking territory for His Kingdom, then we have already made the choice to serve the one whom Scripture calls *the enemy*. Maybe you never consciously decided to serve either God or the devil. Trust me, many people haven't. But as the saying goes, "Failing to plan means planning to fail." In this case, failing to choose God—or to choose *life* (as Moses told the Israelites)—is the same as choosing to serve the evil one. Be sure you choose life!

CHAPTER FIVE

Exposing Jezebel and Delilah Spirits—Destroyers of the Church

Principality Spirits on the Prowl

I would like to start off by making it clear to everyone that the two demons discussed in this chapter will never be more powerful than our Lord Jesus Christ.

So we should ask ourselves, why are these two principalities—Jezebel and Delilah—bringing down churches today? That is a good and honest question, and I would like to shed some light on the reason why. Many of the churches today (thank God not all) are in bed with these two demons, one way or another. These churches are busy teaching and preaching Jesus, but they are not hearing Jesus teach them. My heart cries out even saying this, but many churches today are *ichabod*, meaning the glory of God has left the church. How sad for that to be said of any church today, and we are not even concerned about it.

Jezebel and Delilah are bringing down ministries of all sizes. Many megachurches have fallen and closed down because these spirits have infiltrated the house of God, and we don't even know how to cast them out and keep them out. We don't even realize they have come in until we see the aftermath of the destruction they leave behind.

Jezebel: Control and Murder

To understand the spirit of Jezebel, we must understand the genesis of this personality in the Bible. The first mention of Jezebel is the rebellion and manipulation done by the wife of King Ahab. It was actually this spirit operating through Queen Jezebel that caused the nation of Israel to turn away from God.

Jezebel carries a spirit of murder; Queen Jezebel killed over one hundred of God's prophets. It is no different in the times we are in today:—the Jezebel spirit is still killing (spiritually) God's leaders in the Church. Bear in mind that the spirit which produced Jezebel's existence, before its nickname was born, we refer to as a "she"; however this spirit is without gender. It can come through a female or male. It comes to kill, steal, and destroy. The number one objective and sign of a Jezebel spirit is that it comes as a controlling spirit but camouflages itself as a godly servant of the Lord.

In the days of old, this spirit dominated and controlled over 450 false prophets. This goes to show you the power that this spirit carries. This same demon is sitting in our churches today. Not only does this spirit captivate the pulpit and have our nation by the throat, it also operates through politicians, governments, mass media, literature, and entertainment. It controls the Internet, social media, radio, and television, through the filth of these channels of the airways. I am shedding light on this principality called Jezebel because my main focus is to expose her in the Church and teach the Church the signs that follow her, before she destroys your ministry and your life. This is my assignment from the Lord.

Delilah, Jezebel's Sidekick

There is another spirit that works side by side with Jezebel: the spirit of Delilah. This spirit has almost the same attributes as Jezebel, but is more subtle than a serpent and more cunning. It comes as a seducing spirit. It has seduced many of our leaders in our churches today and brought them down to nothing. To understand the spirit of Delilah, we must go back to the genesis of this personality in the Bible. The first mention of Delilah is in the book of Judges, chapter 16. This spirit is a fornicating, adulterous spirit, and it seduces a man or woman who is anointed by God to commit these acts in the church.

It is a spirit that knows how to vex you until it breaks you and steals your anointing. Like Jezebel, it strips your anointing and then kills the anointed person. It is sad, but you don't even know when it is happening. Look at the case of Samson, a man handpicked by God from birth who had an incredible anointing on his life. This anointing was his strength. However, he never heeded God's warnings, and he ended up in the hands of this principality called Delilah. You know how the story ends, and it wasn't pretty.

The Jezebel and Delilah spirits flow largely unhindered throughout the Church today. These spirits flaunt themselves in our churches day and night, night and day, and across the world today, in the entertainment and fashion industries, in our schools and colleges. Where can you go in society that the influences of Jezebel and Delilah spirits are not felt? They are destroyers of our culture and society, and if we don't identify and remove these two principalities and know their attributes and how they infiltrate the house of God, how then can we help set the captives free in this world today?

Here are the twenty-one telltale traits of these two spirits for our ministries and our churches:

1. Bring fear (caused Elijah to run)

2. Attack ministers

3. Attack the anointing and those anointed

4. Only do their own will, never God's

5. Give the appearance of repentance, then they attack

6. Need to be praised, elevated; they worship themselves and get others to praise them

7. Have a possessive love to destroy and control

8. Are loyal until you disagree with them—then they rebel against you

9. Do all that is asked of them, as long as it is according to their overall plan

10. Plant seeds of discord in others that often lead to conflict or even division in a church

11. Use others to carry out their evil plans

12. Work alone; they only use others

13. Have their own agenda, never God's or other people's

14. Do not listen to God's voice or anyone else's

15. Are very religious: "I heard from God, and He spoke to me."

16. Seek positions of authority in order to control, discredit, and reach their goal

17. Are not committed to anyone

18. Seek affirmation and significance

19. Have illegitimate authority

20. Are convincing liars

21. Rebel when corrected

Warning: The goal of the Jezebel and/or Delilah spirit is to destroy leaders, ministries, and nations. So let's stop being a gentleman with the devil and his kingdom.

Everyone in the Church can learn to identify these two spirits. We pray against them, we fast, but we go into spiritual warfare the wrong way. That's why we can never get the victory in the battle. Without Jezebel there is no Ahab, and without Ahab there is no Jezebel. The devil knows this. For us as believers to win the war, we must discern the battle before we engage. Many times we engage but we never discern, and so we lose the fight. This doesn't mean that our God is not all-powerful—He is and always will be—but so many believers don't know how to discern the battle these days. How can we confront something when we don't know how to discern it? The devil knows that the Church is lacking in discernment and takes advantage of us. The apostle Paul warned us: "lest Satan should get an advantage of us: for we are not ignorant of his devices" (2 Cor. 2:11).

As a diversion, the devil gets our attention by having us focus too quickly on Jezebel or Delilah. The first spirit that attacks a church, long before Jezebel comes in, is the spirit of Ahab, over the church leadership. Why would Ahab come in before Jezebel? I'm glad you asked. The reason is that Ahab is the only spirit that can tolerate Jezebel, and that is a description of the leadership of today that is tolerating Jezebel in our churches.

The effect of this demon is to flood the soul of the leadership with weakness and fear. That's the nature of the Ahab spirit: to give his authority over to Jezebel. Another thing to note is that the Ahab spirit occupies areas of tolerance within the mind of the woman or man who is in leadership; this is most dangerous. This spirit operates the same way with the spirit of Delilah.

The spirit of Samson will take over the leadership before Delilah is ushered in. The attributes of a Samson spirit are anger, unforgiveness, control, and disobedience. When leaders operate under these conditions, this spirit has attacked them.

One of the testimonies I've heard is that Jezebel puts a black veil, so to speak, over the leadership's spiritual eyes so they won't see her coming. In order to gain power and authority over the leaders and anyone working there, the Jezebel spirit will manipulate herself into the hearts of the leadership and discredit those who are in her way, those who are working for that ministry.

Delilah, on the other hand, will seduce the leader of that ministry, or anyone close to the leader, into fornication or adultery. If these spirits are not discerned in time, they will destroy that ministry.

There are three "weapons of mass destruction" that the Church needs today, but which the Church has largely failed to recognize. With these weapons we can be constantly on the offense against the kingdom of darkness. The first weapon is a powerful *intercessory team* that has a spirit of unity attached to it. The second weapon is a team of *spiritual warfare intercessors*, and the third weapon is a team of *deliverance ministers*. We'll go deeper into these weapons in a later chapter.

Summary

This is how we will win the battle, by identifying the patterns of these two demonic, so-called "sisters" of Satan's unholy kingdom, to bring them down to nothing.

CHAPTER
SIX

The Devil's Religions

While we're on the subject of the devil's craftiness and deceit, you should know that he created the word *religion*. He established his kingdom through different religions, except Christianity—even though for two thousand-plus years he's tried to dilute or pollute it. Today, the enemy is in fact working through these other religions. This is another way he steals your identity.

I want to expose the devil for who he is through the religions he has established on the earth, as well as the demons in the spirit realm that are working behind the scenes.

Islam

First let's talk about Islam, a religion that calls itself a "religion of peace." During Ramadan, Muslims fast morning and evening for thirty days. They pray five times a day and attend their services in the mosque. The Koran, which was written by a murderous spirit, talks about infidels, and if you were to become a Muslim and then convert to a different religion, the Koran commands that you be murdered. Muslims torture their victims to the point of no return. They even take their own lives (which is a suicide spirit) in the name of Allah—who (in my opinion as a former Satan worshiper) is no god at all, but a demonic principality. In fact, in my former days I had a spiritual contract with the demonic principality named Zarabanda (an African name) that reigns over the Middle East. The favorite color of Zarabanda is green. If you go look at the mosque in Mecca, the most common color you see on their doors and flags is green. Then how is it that this religion of "peace" can get you to Heaven?

New Age

How the devil has stolen the minds of those who practice this occult. He has brainwashed them into worshiping everything and anything that has been created and to believe in it with a counterfeit faith. What keeps them away from the truth? Why would they want to worship created things when they can worship the Creator who created those things? They have been hit by a delusional and delirious spirit, to think that putting their faith in created things and nature will get them to Heaven.

There is a demonic book out there that speaks half-truths (which is no truth at all). You can feel the demons jump off the pages when reading this book. Through these writings these demons can steal your identity and destiny.

Here is an example, from the book entitled *The Secret*. This is a book based on the Law of Attraction, which is said to determine the complete order of the universe and of our personal lives through the process of "like attracts like." The author claims that as we think and feel, a corresponding frequency is sent out into the universe that attracts back to us events and circumstances on that same frequency. For example, if you think angry thoughts and feel angry, it is claimed that you will attract back events and circumstances that cause you to feel more anger. Conversely, if you think and feel positively, you will attract back positive events and circumstances. Actually, feeling anger (in this example) *only* goes out to the spirit realm, and it gets the attention of the devil and demons, which gives them legal rights over your words and emotions, and all you bring back is an attack of hell on your life.

Proponents of this "law" claim that simply changing one's thoughts and feelings can attract desirable outcomes such as health, wealth, and happiness. For example, some people believe that using this "secret" can cure cancer. This is pure deception. The devil counterfeits the Kingdom of Jesus Christ and creates false healings by first afflicting the person with a disease and then removing it.

The book of Job shows how the enemy afflicted Job with painful boils from head to toe. Only the Lord was able to heal him, not the devil. But the devil tries to mimic God, as always, so what the devil does is afflict the person with a disease for a season and then stops afflicting them for another season. The person goes back to normal and calls this a healing, but it's no healing at all. This keeps them in demonic bondage with the enemy, as he now has legal rights to continue to afflict this person whenever he wants.

As Proverbs 18:21 states, "The tongue has the power of life and death, and those who love it will eat its fruit." The Bible says to speak life; the enemy uses the counterfeit by using the law of attraction to bring death. This is a counterfeit light like good karma or bad karma, which is demonic. One of the things I learned in the enemy's camp is that I had the power to attract people through their negative words. As God says in Deuteronomy 30:19:

> *Today I have given you the choice between life and death, between blessings and curses. Now I call on Heaven and earth to witness the choice you make. Oh, that you would choose life, so that you and your descendants might live!* (Deut. 30:19 NLT)

Santeria

Santeria...what a joke. The word *Santeria* means the worship of saints. Right off the bat they are deceiving you and pointing the finger in the wrong direction, because the only one they should be worshiping is Jesus Christ. From the very beginning they are misleading you. There are no saints at all; they are demons. The foundation of their religion is based on five main gods, which they call *Reachers*. These are their names: Obatala, Yemaya, Ochun, Chango, and Oya.

These are five demonic principalities. They have given themselves these names, have deceived millions with their big deception because they infiltrate culture this way, and Santeria is one of the most powerful occult religions on the earth today. I lived that life for twenty-five years.

What a mockery this religion is; I despise Santeria. I love the people, but I hate the religion. They dress themselves in white for 365 days after their ceremony called *Santo*. They claim that dressing in white means purity. How is it that white clothes means purity? How do white clothes make the person pure? Purity should come from within the person, and the only way that can happen is through salvation through Jesus Christ. They also abstain from different types of food. How silly is this, because the demons told them so. The warnings, if you don't do this, are that you can pass away and be terminally ill and end up in the hospital. My question to them is, if the demon says stay away from drinking milk and eating eggs and rice or else you will die, but you have eaten eggs and rice and drunk milk for forty years and never died, explain this one?

These people are under a controlling spirit: a spirit of fear and torment. To make another point, these demons, the so-called Reachers, also force the people to stay away from wearing certain colors. For example, they can't wear a red, blue, yellow, or black dress, suit, T-shirt, or sweatshirt because something evil can happen to them if they do. How is it that from a child you have been wearing all these colors and nothing happened? Those that practice this religion should reflect on these facts and not be deceived. This is foolishness—God made all colors for us to enjoy!

Catholicism

From my perspective as a former follower of Santeria (which is the worship of saints), Catholicism is the worship of the saints, which are idols, and the worship of Mary. How is it that you can confess your sins to man and your sins are forgiven, or pray to statues and they take your prayers to the Lord? How is it that saying three Hail Mary's and three Our Father's forgives our sins? How is it that praying the rosary gets you closer to God? What is this place called Purgatory, as the Scripture says in 2 Corinthians 5:8: "We are confident, I say, and willing rather to be absent from the body, and to be present with the Lord." As well, Jesus told the thief on the Cross, in Luke 23:43: "I assure you, today you will be with me in Paradise" (NLT). Jesus said Paradise, not Purgatory.

Spiritualism/Palo Mayombe

This is another joke; how they deceive their people. They throw these big demonic feasts where people get demon-possessed and the demons use their bodies to communicate with people in the feasts. They channel spirits—the so-called mediums—and these demons come down through their bodies. The first thing demons ask for is white or dark rum and a cigar. They smoke cigars and drink all night while possessing the people. And then the demons have the audacity to say to the same people that they shouldn't go to the bars, clubs, or any house parties or drink any kind of liquor because it's not good for them!

These demons even prohibit their followers from smoking cigars and cigarettes. What a lie. In the feast they can use you to do these things and it's OK, but not in your own leisure time. You are told not to because something bad can happen to you. This is deception. The only reason these demons do that is because they want your body to stay healthy so they can abuse you. I know this because I lived in that world for twenty-five years. They also use animals to "cleanse" you from your sins, which is another lie. The only person who can cleanse you from your sins is the Son of God. Santeria is a religion of lies. People are captivated by it like a whirlwind, and their life is controlled to the point that it doesn't belong to them anymore. How easy the enemy steals their identity.

Tarot Cards

For the many people who like to get their tarot cards read, let me expose this deception, since I used to read tarot cards when I was in that world. Tea leaves and cups are the same thing. The readers operate the same way. They promise to tell you your future. They break the cards in three piles: past, present, and future. They tell you your past to amaze you, they tell you your present to captivate you. These readings are actually done by familiar spirits—demons that walk the earth, assigned to each person to become "familiar" with them. The Bible exposes them. Now these demons are going to tell you your future. They may say you will have a car accident, or they can see you getting a divorce, or they see one of your children is going to get sick, or they see how you're going to get a great job. Your response is, "My husband loves me" or "I love my husband," or "My family and children are healthy." The spirits will then say for you to wait and see, that these things are going to happen.

The devil doesn't know the future. But little do you know that the demon speaking through the card reader and telling you all these things is the demon you are taking home with you, and he will make all these things happen. Then out of desperation you will run back into the hands of the devil (through the spiritualist) and say, "Oh, everything you said to me happened!" The spiritualist will say to you, "I can fix those things for you and make them go away for a fee of $_____." Out of pure deception you will pay that fee, and the medium will call back the demon and your life will temporarily go back to normal. But you now have a demonic door opened in your life and the life of your family that the devil can walk in and out of anytime he wants. You have cursed your family down to the third and fourth generation as it says in Exodus 20:4:

> *You must not make for yourself an idol of any kind or an image of anything in the heavens or on the earth or in the sea. You must not bow down to them or worship them, for I, the Lord your God, am a jealous God who will not tolerate your affection for any other gods. I lay the sins of the parents upon their children; the entire family is affected—even children in the third and fourth generations of those who reject me* (NLT).

Jehovah's Witnesses

This is another avenue Satan uses to steal your life. They fabricated their own "Bible." They believe that Jesus is not the Son of God, but that he is a god. They don't believe in the Trinity or that the Holy Spirit is a person. They believe the Holy Spirit is like electricity—just power, but not a person of the trinity.

I know these things to be true because my mother was a Jehovah's Witness for eight years. I saw my mother get sick in a restaurant and be rushed to the hospital because she was allergic to seafood. Five times that evening she almost died. But the Lord Jesus Christ used that opportunity to reveal Himself to my mother that evening. I remember clearly that none of the

Jehovah's Witnesses came to the hospital to pray for my mother. All the Christian believers rushed to my mother's side, knowing that she was a Jehovah's Witness. That evening the hospital room was undeniably filled with the presence of the Lord. And that night my mother gave her life to the Lord. She took back her identity that had been stolen for eight years. Thank God for Jesus Christ and His great mercy!

Summary

These are some of the many religions the enemy uses to rob you from God's best in your life. Thank God that He has made a way through His Son Jesus Christ and you don't have to stay in bondage or shackles when you can be free.

CHAPTER SEVEN

Fighting Back Through Spiritual Warfare

All my life I've been fighting. I am always fighting for a cause, whether a belief system, an opportunity, a chance in life, a job, or fighting for my family.

Even on the dark side, for twenty-five years, I was always fighting against anything that opposed the kingdom of darkness, especially against the Christian believers. But today, thanks be to God, I am on the right side and have been given the opportunity to be enlisted in the most prestigious spiritual army in all eternity.

Sometimes I sit back and look through the portals of my past and examine the fights, battles, and wars of my life. People from the dark side, from the demonic kingdom I was once loyal to, fought to the very end to take over regions, control neighborhoods, and take control of the people in these neighborhoods and regions, yet for a cost that was dead in the water from the very beginning—with no eternal rewards of any kind. When it was all said and done, the only place we were entitled to was hell.

Today, as a believer in Christ Jesus, I ask myself this question over and over: Why are Christians not fighting back? The biggest concerns of too many churches today are growth programs and how many ministries they have in one building; most churches are just preaching people happy. I can imagine how this grieves the heart of God because it grieves mine and I am only a human being—how much more must it grieve God, since He is a holy God.

He is also a God of war, especially against the hosts of hell. In the matter of spiritual warfare, Christ has clearly won the victory. However, He leaves it up to us, His Church, to enforce that victory. We see this principle after Christ rose from the dead. Jesus appeared to His disciples and said,

> *All authority in heaven and on earth has been given to Me. Therefore go and make disciples of all nations, baptizing them in the name of the Father and of the Son and of the Holy Spirit, and teaching them to obey everything I have commanded you* (Matt. 28:18-20 NIV).

Christ died for all the churches on the planet, regardless of denomination. It's time to assemble to fight back and reclaim what the devil has stolen from the Church, from our neighborhoods, from our families, from our marriages, from our schools, from our businesses, and from our very own lives. I am not asking for people to fight back in the natural or to hate anyone, because everything that confronts us is supernatural. "For the weapons of our warfare are not carnal, but mighty through God to the pulling down of strong holds" (2 Cor. 10:4).

Christian business owners today work very hard to be self-employed and sacrifice. They don't cut corners and they are truly honest; they even cut back on family vacations and gatherings, or other nice activities, so they can give to build their businesses as they provide for their families and become successful business owners. But then the devil unleashes homosexual spirits to stir up that community (they call it an "alternative lifestyle"), to provoke Christian business owners to compromise their faith and go against God because a customer wants a wedding cake or a photographer or a wedding planner, or even a place to hold their same-sex ceremony. And all we do is sit back and do nothing about this? It's time to fight back spiritually and engage the hosts of hell.

Another thing I ask myself is this: How is it that the atheist community has so much control? Because most Americans want to say "In God We Trust" and sing our national anthem, and we want our children to be grateful in school and pray over their lunches. Yet if one of our kids turns in an essay with the name of Jesus in it, the school pressures the kid to change it; they threaten our child with an "F" if he doesn't remove Jesus' name. If they wear a T-shirt announcing who they believe in—the Lord Jesus Christ—they get sent home from school. This is purely demonic. It's time to fight back!

How crazy it is in the corporate world, I think. We believers give our all in the workplace, we don't murmur or complain, and we work twice as hard, not only for that company, but we work unto the Lord. Yet we can't even take off Good Friday because it's a mockery to them. Even in the workplace, if someone sneezes and you reply with "God Bless you," they might threaten you with losing your job. But someone can curse, bad-mouth other people, and sleep around with anyone they want and the company is OK with this.

Colleges are brainwashing our children to believe in a system that is straight from the pit of hell. They try to make our children believe that God does not exist, that you only have to reason with yourself about what is right and what is wrong, and that God is just a fairytale. This is so demonic that even a Christian movie was made about this very issue. The schools are even handing out demonic flyers to the schoolchildren. If you agree with one of these flyers, it is like buying a ticket to hell. Atheistic professors want the students to believe, live, and act like they themselves do. They think the world owes them something, and they threaten our children by telling them that, as soon as they walk in those college doors, they (our children) don't have a say over what they believe in or who they are. Our children are being threatened in ways that will affect their education.

It's time to take a stand. I have experienced this myself with my own daughter, but the devil is a liar, and he made a great mistake and picked the wrong kid to mess with, because her daddy knows how to pray and touch Heaven on her behalf. Her daddy knows spiritual warfare.

The foundation of marriage has a crack in it, caused by groups that don't believe in the sanctity of marriage anymore.

They say that when you love someone, that love is love, and with their narrow-minded thinking they have managed to get their way. It is sad to say, but we have compromised the unity of marriage, which God created from the beginning of time. Where is the Church today? We can preach about marriage in the church building, we can teach about it in the church building, but outside of the four walls of the church building we are silent because we are being threatened by the minority—that they will take away our nonprofit 501c3 status.

Back in the day when I was growing up, there was a saying for people who were practicing the alternative lifestyle. They would say, "I'm out of the closet." By the looks of today, they are all out of the closet and the Western Church has run into the closet. We the Church run into the closet and hide, and we do nothing about the problem. I thank God that not all churches are in the closet, that there are still those that speak forth and stand up for righteousness and holiness. Thank God, I belong to one of those churches.

It's time to come out of the closet, as a church, and engage the enemy. It's time to fight back for the family, marriage, Christian business owners, our workplaces, our schools and colleges, our neighborhoods and communities, and to take back our regions, the government, and the country as a whole. It's time to fight back for the backsliders, to bring them home. So, devil: we are putting you on notice.

Pinpointing Targets

Many times I have been asked the ultimate question, "What is spiritual warfare?" In other words, how do you fight against the devil and his demons? Whether in a television interview, radio show, at a conference, or some other event, without a doubt this question always comes up.

What I would like to share with you is how to bring down targets in the enemy's camp that are tormenting or plaguing believers today. Many good Christian brothers and sisters love the Lord, but they don't know how to fight spiritually. Spiritual warfare isn't influenced by how many times we attend church, or how long we have been saved (as good as those things are). Spiritual warfare has to have a foundation and a structure in order for us to fight and win the battles against the kingdom of darkness.

The number one key we need to establish in spiritual warfare is the fear of the Lord. "The fear of the Lord is the beginning of wisdom, and knowledge of the Holy One is understanding" (Prov. 9:10 NIV). This is where spiritual warfare begins and ends.

Yet the fear of the Lord seems to be lacking in most of our churches today. I am sure that it blows the minds of angels and even of demons so much that they stand in amazement at our lack of fear and reverence for God. "You believe that there is one God. You do well. Even the demons believe—and tremble!" (James 2:19 NKJV).

This is why, when it comes to spiritual warfare, the majority of the time we believers never get the victory. The deception of Satan throughout the portals of time, all the way back to the Garden of Eden, is to break the fear of the Lord in your life. This has been the most effective tool that Satan has used to tower over the Church.

In the Garden of Eden the devil managed, as he is doing today, to bring the lies that will strip you down and take the fear of God out of your life. When he told Eve, "Eat of this tree... you will not surely die," he was saying, "You do not have to fear

God." God gave a commandment, but Adam and Eve totally disobeyed Him and believed the devil instead. Most of us have fallen into the same trap today, because we have been taught by our church that God is a big Daddy sitting in Heaven, and that He will not refuse His children if we pray a certain way or with endless demands and claims and request for all sorts of things from Him. Countless preachers have preached those messages over and over.

We have lost our way: The way of the fear of the Lord. The Word says that the fear of the Lord is the beginning of wisdom, so if you don't fear the Lord, then how can you fight and win against the attacks of the enemy over your life?

The fear of the Lord means to reverence Him, to be in awe of who He is. He is a holy God, and He cannot be compared to anyone or anything. The longer I walk with the Lord, the more I realize my total helplessness: That I am nothing and can do nothing on my own, and that anything accomplished in my life is by the hands of the Lord and Him alone. This is the fear of the Lord. As believers, we should have this reverence engraved in our spirits and hearts. We should live by this; otherwise, Satan will always have us by the throat. The fear of the Lord is the beginning of spiritual warfare.

Breaking Strongholds: Self-Deliverance

A self-deliverance simply means that people reading this today can be set free of demons, in Jesus's name.

Demons cannot enter into the spirit of a Christian because the spirit of a Christian is sealed until the day of redemption (see Eph. 4:30), but any other area that is not 100 percent surrendered to the Holy Spirit—or where there is a legal right for demons to enter because of sins committed—can be occupied by unclean spirits until we cast these devils out in Jesus's name.

A demon is an unclean spirit that is looking for a body to live in, and they are able to enter people through personal and generational sins and the following doorways:

- Personal and generational sins

- Curses

- Dabbling in the occult

- Witchcraft

- Alcohol

- Smoking marijuana and using any kinds of psychotropic drugs

- Pornography

- Worldly movies and music

- Having occult objects in your house

- Sex outside of marriage

- Abortions

- Incest

- Rape

- Unforgiveness

- Being angry and letting the sun go down on your wrath

These are some of the main doorways through which these unclean spirits enter. They enter into people and will reside in the flesh, which is your physical body and soul (your mind, will, and emotions).

Again, I repeat to Christian believers (those who are living a life surrendered to Jesus Christ): Demons cannot enter into our spirit because our spirit is sealed with the Holy Spirit until the day of redemption (see Eph. 4:30). But any other area that is not 100 percent surrendered to the Holy Spirit, or where there is a legal right for demons to enter through sins we have committed, can be occupied and tormented by unclean spirits until we renounce and repent and break those legal rights and cast these devils out in Jesus Christ's name.

Deliverance was one-third of Jesus Christ's ministry and the first sign that Jesus said would follow those who believe in Him: "these signs shall follow them that believe; in my name shall they cast out devils; they shall speak with new tongues..." (Mark 16:17).

We have authority in Jesus Christ over the power of the enemy to cast out devils in Jesus' name. Here are a few verses to prove this:

And I will give unto thee the keys of the Kingdom of Heaven: and whatsoever thou shalt bind on earth shall be bound in Heaven: and whatsoever thou shalt loose on earth shall be loosed in Heaven (Matt. 16:19).

Verily I say unto you, Whatsoever ye shall bind on earth shall be bound in Heaven: and whatsoever ye shall loose on earth shall be loosed in Heaven (Matt. 18:18).

Then He called His twelve disciples together, and gave them power and authority over all devils, and to cure diseases (Luke 9:1).

Behold, I give unto you power to tread on serpents and scorpions, and over all the power of the enemy: and nothing shall by any means hurt you (Luke 10:19).

Now we are ready to begin with your self-deliverance.

I want you to cough deeply out of your stomach, and then just relax and breathe naturally.

Demons are spirits, and they often exit the body as tears, coughs, burps, yawns, screams, gas, or vomit. So you might need a tissue or to have a garbage can close by and use them as needed, and remember: every demon out is one less in.

There is nothing to be afraid of, as they are going to come out of you today in Jesus Christ's name. Just breathe regularly and let them go, in Jesus Christ's name.

Alright, here we go:

Self-Deliverance Prayer

Right now, in Jesus Christ's name, I bind up and rebuke any strongman and all unclean spirits working inside or against me.

I bind the gatekeeper and bind all hindering spirits and demonic reinforcements from interfering with this deliverance in Jesus Christ's name.

In Jesus Christ's name I bind up all the principalities, powers of the air, all demonic kingdoms, dominions, thrones, and every demonic entity and unclean spirit working against me and my family.

I put you on notice, Satan that I am attacking you from my position of authority seated with the Lord Jesus Christ in the Highest of the Heavenlies.

I loose warrior angels of God to surround me right now, and I ask you, Father God, to loose a wall of fire like in Zechariah 2:5 to surround me and my family right now, in Jesus Christ's name.

I loose warrior angels with swords to go into the lowest portion of my body and surround me and to separate all demons from the strongman and each other and spoil the demons of their power, armor, rank, and resources, in Jesus Christ's name.

I loose the sword of the Lord to cut off all connections between the demons on the inside and the fallen angels and unclean spirits on the outside, in Jesus Christ's name.

I execute the judgments written on all devils inside right now, and I loose the judgments of God along with fire and burning and destruction perpetual on all the devils attacking me right now, in Jesus Christ's name and in accordance with Psalm 149:9.

I loose angels of God into attack formation and to attack all foul spirits inside of me! Charge! In Jesus Christ's name.

Every unclean spirit that the Lord Jesus Christ wants to come out of me: come out now, and go to where the Lord Jesus Christ is sending you!

All spirits of insecurity—inferiority—every type of fear—nervousness—anxiety—insomnia:
Come out in Jesus Christ's name!

Wounded spirit—deep, wounded hurt—abandonment—orphan spirt—trauma—superstition spirits:
Come out in Jesus Christ's name!

Spirit of heaviness—depression—hopelessness—worry—sadness—isolation—suicide:
Come out in Jesus Christ's name!

Every spirit of cigarettes—alcohol—nicotine—marijuana—gluttony—eating disorders—rebellion—cursing—foul mouth—all psychotropic drugs and sorcery:
Come out in Jesus Christ's name!

Lying—cheating—murder—revenge—abortions—coveting—slander—mocking—rage—angry man—jealous—deceit:
Come out in Jesus Christ's name!

Anger—rage—resentment—unforgiveness—bitterness—murder—revenge:
Come out in Jesus Christ's name!

Doubt and unbelief—confusion—chaos—antichrist spirits:
Come out in Jesus Christ's name!

Pride—big pride—little pride—stiff necked pride—
ugly pride:
Come out in Jesus Christ's name!

All spirits of witchcraft, idolatry, divination,
necromancy, Ouija board, séance, tarot cards,
consulting with psychics:
Come out in Jesus Christ's name!

Spirits that came in from reiki, yoga, martial arts,
transcendental meditation, reading occult books,
Wicca, Hecate, the Goddess, Freemasonry, eastern
star:
Come out in Jesus Christ's name!

All spirits of Santeria—Palo Mayombe—
Chango—Eckinkar—New Age spirits—another
JESUS—meditation—acupuncture—acupressure—
spiritualism:
Come out in Jesus Christ's name!

I loose the sword of the Lord to cut and chop all
kundalini, python, and serpentine spirits off of my
spine and in my body:
Come out in Jesus Christ's name!

I bind and rebuke all spirits of mind control—occult
mind binding—mind binders—octagon—squid—
oculus—witchcraft mind control.

I break your power and cut all control spirits
connected to my mind, and all matriarchal and

patriarchal control spirits connected to me, in Jesus
Christ's name:
Come out in Jesus Christ's name!

I break and cut all psychic heredity—all lay lines—
all ungodly soul ties connected to me and command
them to:
Come out in Jesus Christ's name!

Spirits that came in through adultery—
incest—rape—fornication—all spirits of
sexual fantasy—incubus—succubus—
Asmodeous—Osmodeous—internet
porn—lust—masturbation—anal
sex—bestiality—homosexuality—sodomy,
I bind and rebuke you and command you to loose
me:
Come out in Jesus Christ's name!

Spirit husband—spirit wife—marriage-
breaking spirits—infidelity—wife
swapping—divorce—frigidity:
Come out in Jesus Christ's name!

All vagabond spirits—hindering spirits—blessing
blockers—religious spirits:
Come out in Jesus Christ's name!

All spirits of sickness, premature death, destruction,
root of bitterness, cancer, asthma, all infirmities:
Come out in Jesus Christ's name!

Father God, I ask you to loose civil war into the demons' camp and cause every demon to attack one another now, in Jesus Christ's name.

*I command my strongman to start throwing out the demons under its command **now**! In Jesus Christ's name.*

I loose the arrows of the Lord God dipped in the blood of Jesus to rain down and impale the demons in Jesus's name.

I loose the hornets of the Lord to sting the demons and drive them out in Jesus Christ's name.

Angels of God! Attack these spirits and cut the strongman away and hook and pull them out in Jesus Christ's name

I loose the fire of God on every demon, in Jesus's name.

I loose fiery destruction on all demons, in Jesus's name.

I loose the fear of the Lord into every demon, in Jesus's name.

Angels of God, burn the demons' scrolls, banners, flags, standards, and seals, and break their cups in Jesus Christ's name.

I rebuke you foul spirits—come out in Jesus Christ's name.

Move! Out! Out! Out! Come out! In Jesus Christ's name.

I am giving you demons a few more seconds to come out and then I am going to cage you up.

Father God, I ask You to loose warrior angels to go in and cage every demon by itself in a cage filled with the blood of our Lord Jesus Christ.

Angels of God, slice these devils, scourge them, read the Word of God to them night and day, and sing the songs from the old Gospel hymnals like "There Is Power in the Blood" until they come out! In Jesus Christ's name.

Demons, I bind you from being able to communicate with one another and you will not harm me or my family in any way. All you can do is come out and confess Jesus Christ as Lord and then go to where the Lord Jesus Christ sends you—never to return.

Keep coming out in Jesus Christ's name!

Angels of God—execute the order in Jesus Christ's name and cage every remaining foul spirit, until next time in deliverance or they release me.

Every demon, as you come out, you are ordered to go to where the Lord Jesus Christ sends you and never return.

I seal this deliverance with the blood of the Lord Jesus Christ. I pray over myself God's spirits of power—love—sound mind—deliverance—health— fear of the lord—grace—mercy—excellent spirit—in Jesus Christ's name.

*Father God, I ask You to send the Holy Spirit now
to fill up every void in me.*

*Bind all demonic backlash—retaliation—revenge
or retribution from attacking me and my family, my
finances, my ministries, my purpose, and my destiny,
In Jesus Christ's name.*

I wrote this chapter as a manual for many people who feel in their hearts that they need deliverance, as many of the churches are not going out on a limb, are not going the extra mile to teach their people and set them free. I pray that this chapter will truly be a blessing to all.

Taking Back your Neighborhood for Jesus Christ

I remember in my former life before Christ as a devil worshiper, I was trained to take over neighborhoods for the devil. The reason why the devil wanted to take over the neighborhood is because his strategy and plan was that if we could take over the neighborhood, we could take over the people. So we would lock down the four corners of the neighborhood, the crossroad streets, which represent the North, South, East and West. Through demonic rituals I was able to accomplish that mission. As believers, we need to take back the neighborhoods out of the hands of the enemy. Why would Jesus Christ place us in certain neighborhoods for a season or sometimes a lifetime? I believe we are called to be the watchmen on the wall to protect and to set the captives free in our neighborhoods, so people can come to the salvation of Jesus Christ.

Step #1 Identify the strongholds in your area. Here are some examples: Witchcraft stores (often called *botanicas)*; mosques (where Muslims worship); psychic reading places; Jehovah's Witnesses temples; centers of dealing drugs, whether a building or street corner.

Step #2 Examine the condition of your area or neighborhood. Do your homework. What is the rate of suicide, the rate of abortion? Is your area a poverty-stricken area? A poverty mindset controls the poverty of the people. See if there are any sex offenders in your area. There is a child molestation spirit and perversion spirit that is trying to ruin our children. If you live in a high-end neighborhood or community, do your homework and look for a self-entitlement spirit, a prideful spirit, a religious spirit, a spirit of antichrist, an atheistic spirit, and an agnostic spirit. Especially if you have colleges or schools in your area, the professors may be wrapped around with these demons. Also look for homosexual clubs, whether in a poverty-stricken neighborhood or rich neighborhood. A racist spirit is a spirit that brings division among cultures. Are there liquor stores in your area? This is an alcohol spirit.

These are some of the many demonic spirits and strongholds that are controlling and hurting people spiritually and keeping them from coming to Christ. It's time to pray spiritual warfare prayers and destroy these targets, uprooting them from your community through effective and consistent prayers.

Also, if Jesus Christ wakes you up at two or three in the morning, these are the best times to pray against these spirits. When I was in the demonic world those were my best hours to be up to do the devil's work. Saints, it's time to take the battle seriously and honor our Lord Jesus Christ. It's time to enforce the victory of the Cross in our neighborhoods.

Summary

Who's watching over your neighborhood: You or the devil? Make an assessment of your neighborhood and take back those areas that have been bound with demonic strongholds. God has put you in that neighborhood for a purpose. People may live and die, spiritually, depending on what you do.

CHAPTER
EIGHT

Destroying the Gates of Hell

We are living in unparalleled times. God is waking up the Church, especially the leadership of the Church at large. Jesus wants the leadership to set themselves up to be armed and dangerous against the enemy of our soul and his wicked devices. I believe that every congregation will follow the leading of the Holy Spirit. I know that for the past decade or so, the Church has been asleep and very unaware of the tactics of the enemy, especially on the subject of spiritual warfare.

The Lord wants to shake us up, raise us up to be ready and to be the end-time Church that He died for; He wants to wake us up to the seriousness of the hour we are living in.

I know that God is speaking to the universal Church; He's graciously doing it. One of the ways He's doing it is by allowing the devil to unleash hell against the Church. Jesus has allowed it to happen to get our attention.

The Body of Christ is experiencing major suffering: broken homes, sickness, mental illness, even spiritual lukewarmness. Many Christians have given up; even pastors are closing down their churches. Fornication spirits, adultery spirits, and many other demonic forces are being unleashed on the Church at large. Thank God not all churches have conformed themselves to the world system. It's time to wake up and be the Church of Jesus Christ. I believe we are in the generation of the Lord's return; we are in the beginning stages. I truly feel this in my spirit because of all the escalations of occult activity, all the rage in Satan's heart today against believers and nonbelievers alike—his rage against all humankind.

I thank God for the Holy Spirit, as He is equipping us to stand in this hour and prevail against the greatest onslaught of demonic attacks that we will ever see in human history. It's important for us as a body of believers that we have the urgency to take our place as the elite army God has raised up for such a time as this. Help us, Lord, to be like the Church in the book of Acts.

I would like to share a passage of Scripture with you. So many times we read this passage and it becomes too familiar and a dullness comes over us, so that we overlook it because we get too comfortable with the Word of God.

> *Finally, be strong in the Lord and in his mighty power. Put on the full armor of God, so that you can take your stand against the devil's schemes. For our struggle is not against flesh and blood, but against*

the rulers, against the authorities, against the powers of this dark world and against the spiritual forces of evil in the heavenly realms. Therefore put on the full armor of God, so that when the day of evil comes, you may be able to stand your ground, and after you have done everything, to stand. Stand firm then, with the belt of truth buckled around your waist, with the breastplate of righteousness in place, and with your feet fitted with the readiness that comes from the gospel of peace. In addition to all this, take up the shield of faith, with which you can extinguish all the flaming arrows of the evil one. Take the helmet of salvation and the sword of the Spirit, which is the word of God (Eph. 6:10-17 NIV).

This is one of the most powerful passages in the New Testament. I would like to share the urgency of how we need to stand on the Word of God. I pray that I am able to bless you and share a portion of it from my heart so that it will equip you with the power of the Holy Spirit to beat down the devil like he deserves: because he stole something from you! Amen. We need to exercise the authority that Jesus Christ has poured into us when He has made it available to us, to destroy the works of darkness.

Finally, my brethren, be strong in the Lord, and in the power of His might (Eph. 6:10 NKJV).

Paul was calling the church at Ephesus to position themselves against the devil and his kingdom. Remember this: We will never win any battle against the enemy if we don't turn to face him. It's not important what the devil throws at you. The importance is what you do afterward: That determines the victory, and knowing who we are in Christ and how we are living in Him. Check yourself and allow me to share with you from the heart. Is your heart on fire for God, or is it cold? Do you have religion, or do you have a relationship with the living God? We need to position ourselves to the pursuit of righteousness and fill our life with the Word of God so that His strength can be imparted into our inner man by the Holy Spirit. So I say to the Church today, be strong in the Lord and make lifestyle changes that please God, so you can carry a powerful anointing.

It's time to take our walk seriously with Christ because too many are allowing the devil to create a false Jesus in their mind. That is idol worship, by the way, because it's not the same Jesus that is in the Bible. Far from it, it is used only to justify the lifestyle that the devil has set up and tricked us into feeling. I say to put on the whole armor of God, so you are able to stand against the schemes and wiles of the devil. We need to live armored lifestyles. This passage from Ephesians is more than a Bible passage. It is a calling, a lifestyle; it's the identity of spiritual warfare of the Church of the living God, if you want to make it in the days to come.

Know this, those of you who are playing patty-cake with the devil: the devil hates you with a rage and fury because you are made in the image of Almighty God. He wants to destroy you; there is no ceasefire and the devil doesn't go on vacation. So rise up, beloved, in whatever situation you find yourself in, and turn to Jesus.

You cannot walk in safety without God. There is a lifestyle and there are choices we need to submit to before we can put on the full armor of God, or the armor won't work. It starts with saying no to the devil and yes to Jesus and getting the Word of

God in us. Then we will be able to stand against the schemes of the evil one. One of the devil's greatest tricks is that he appears to not exist, even to the Church, because we are so caught up in the day-in and day-out events of our lives that we forget there is an enemy out there.

> *Be sober, be vigilant; because your adversary the devil, as a roaring lion, walketh about, seeking whom he may devour* (1 Pet. 5:8).

As believers, we can lose the sense of urgency of the spiritual fight and only realize it when it's too late and the devil is already on our doorstep. We lose sight of the reality of this creature called the devil, who wants to destroy us. Satan is a spiritual being filled with anger, and he will not stop at any cost. He is after our life-purpose and our destiny. Many believers have died premature deaths because they have taken this monster lightly. I heard a great preacher say once that "the richest place in the whole earth is the cemetery." Why? Because many believers died prematurely, with their purpose and destiny unfulfilled because they had stepped out of the permissive will of God, and the devil destroyed them. That is sad to say, when Jesus Christ died to set us free.

With sadness in my heart, I hear many Christians say, "I am very busy with my work and family, and God understands." The devil, on the other hand, doesn't care about any of that stuff. It's funny; these Christians think the devil is saying, "Well, you know, let me give you a week off; I won't attack you; I'll cut you a break." He will destroy you in a heartbeat. In the midst of you saying "God understands," know this: the devil has no mercy on any true believer, whether today or tomorrow. He has great power and he is invisible. So wake up, Church. You will never defeat him with your own strength. God is calling us to stand up and fight a real battle against the eternal enemy of our soul.

Ephesians 6:12 says, "For our struggle is not against flesh and blood, but against the rulers, against the authorities, against the powers of this dark world and against the spiritual forces of evil in the heavenly realms."

What a powerful revelation. Amazing, the insight and advantage Paul shares with us in this passage. I would like to outline four levels of hierarchy of Satan's kingdom. These four names are spiritual powers. Remember, there are many levels of Satan's kingdom, and they all run in order: different levels of authority and powers. In order to overcome those Satanic powers we need to live righteous lives and a life of prayer, so we can resist these dark powers that are aiming for us every day. If we don't live for Jesus Christ we are opening doors, portals, and gateways to the kingdom or darkness. The Bible makes it clear that the *ear gate*, the *eye gate*, and the *mouth gate* are entries that, if unguarded, the devil has legal access to so he can wreak havoc in our life.

> *The lust of the flesh and the lust of the eyes, and the pride of life, is not of the Father, but is of the world* (1 John 2:16).

I want to give you a warning that what you watch on television, in the movies, music, video games, entertainment, and the Internet (all forms of media) are some of the devil's tools, as the Bible says that the devil is the prince of the air. A short way of saying this Scripture passage is that it means the devil controls these gateways. Even the cartoons are filled with occult activity. The most innocent (so-called) movies are filled with garbage that will dull your mind to mush. There is no way, after watching it, that you can say you have the mind of Christ, as the devil now has legal rights into your mind.

These degrading acts and filthy language contaminate our spirit and weaken us down to nothing. This is a setup from the pits of hell. As an ex-devil worshiper, I used to entice Christians to engage in these degrading acts, to bring them to their flesh, to destroy them spiritually and ultimately physically. Guard yourself from these attacks. Remember, we are wrestling with supernatural powers and evil forces, so we need supernatural weapons to defeat them in Jesus' name alone.

Too many churches today are trying to fight the devil on his own territory and with natural weapons that will never win the battle. The Lord is calling the Church to fight in a supernatural way. Ephesians 6:13 tells us, "Therefore take up the whole armor of God, that you may be able to withstand in the evil day, and having done all, to stand" (NKJV). In other words, be on guard.

In this passage in Ephesians, when he was chained up in prison to a Roman solider, Paul listed six different facets of the soldier's armor. It is amazing how the Holy Spirit gave Paul revelation into the spirit realm by using the Roman solider and the armor he was dressed in.

The *helmet of salvation* is having the mind of Christ protect us, and not allowing the devil to invade our mind and bombard it with thoughts of the past or anything we are struggling with in the present. Never allow yourself to dwell on the situations in your mind. "Casting down arguments and every high thing that exalts itself against the knowledge of God" (2 Cor. 10:5 NKJV). Be steadfast and pray in the spirit to win and take back your mind.

The helmet of salvation protects your mind against the enemy attacks and keeps your mind on things above instead of the circumstance you find yourself in.

The *breastplate of righteousness* symbolically means to know our identity in Christ. We also need to guard our hearts, having a pure heart—genuinely to serve God, and to fear and obey God—and having pure hands to deal with the things of God with honesty and integrity.

The *belt of truth* is standing on guard, being a person of prayer. It costs something to be a person of prayer. Many Christians struggle to have a prayer closet and they find prayer boring. The devil gets excited over this. Jesus was the greatest example of a man of prayer. It's time to pray. Don't allow the enemy to steal your prayer life.

The *sword of the spirit* is the Word of God. This sword is crucial whether you are on the mountaintop or in the valley, because you can encounter the devil at any given time. Many of us miss it, and we are walking around drained, with no spiritual growth because we are not filled with the Word of God and our inner man is spiritually anemic. In this spiritual condition, the devil has a field day with us and that should not be.

The *shoes of peace* means walking in the straight path that Jesus has set us on. Matthew 7:13-14 says,

> *Enter by the narrow gate; for wide is the gate and broad is the way that leads to destruction, and there are many who go in by it. Because narrow is the gate and difficult is the way which leads to life, and there are few who find it* (NKJV).

When you stand on this Scripture and believe God 100 percent, you are wearing the right pair of shoes. Then you will not be moved out of your purpose and destiny.

The *shield of faith* is used to stand strong against the fiery darts of the enemy. In other words, it doesn't matter what life throws at you. It doesn't matter what circumstance you find yourself in or what the devil says to you or what witch tries to hex you. If your shield of faith is in place, I can only describe it in these words: Any ship can ride out any storm as long as the water doesn't get in. It is the same with us; we can ride out any attack as long as the attack doesn't get in us. Please listen to me: It's not what the devil throws at you, it's what you do with it when it comes your way.

In the days we live in, we need to be more determined than the enemy. Pray and ask the Lord, "Lord, give me the spirit of prayer," so your inner man can be renewed daily and touched by God. The only way we can have this incredible blessing is by making lifestyle changes. Are you aware, beloved, that the enemy knows this so well, like the back of his hand? That's why he makes it his business to keep us busy. We think that being busy makes us productive, but in actuality it keeps us away from the prayer closet. Many times we are tired, lazy, and even sleepy. It's so important to keep watch over our spiritual life, the one that we have to give God an account for. Please hear me on this: Satan laughs, even applauds, when we are too busy living for the flesh, but I've got good news for you: "He who sins is of the devil, for the devil has sinned from the beginning. For this purpose the Son of God was manifested, that He might destroy the works of the devil" (1 John 3:8 NKJV).

Our God is a God of war. God's heart is set on destroying the works of Satan's kingdom. I don't understand why the Church tolerates the very things that God hates. The Church finds itself in bed with the devil, but Jesus came to destroy the devil and his cronies. God has vengeance in his heart to destroy every aspect of the enemy's kingdom with a rage and fury, doing this through His Church—whether it's spirits of sickness, divorce, tormenting spirits, spirits of wickedness, homosexuality, any and every principality and every territorial demon, starting from the second and first heaven all the way down to the earth.

Every marine spirit needs to be dealt with, not with white gloves, but with the heart of Jesus Christ, that has zero tolerance against the devil's kingdom. We are soldiers of the greatest army you will ever find or that you can even imagine in your lifetime, and the devil knows it well. We know it as the Church of Jesus Christ. I'm calling every believer to fight, fight, fight and never give up, through prayer, fasting, and mixing your faith with the Word of God. Stand strong in Christ and Christ alone. Never let the devil take over your mind or lock your heart. Let it be quickened by the Holy Spirit of God. Let us stop playing patty-cake with the devil and be radical for Jesus Christ. The Church started that way in the book of Acts, and I know in my heart we will finish that way because our God is the same yesterday, today, and forever more.

Be watchful to the end with perseverance. It's time to wake up and put hell on notice. Let's stop taking the devil lightly. He is the number one enemy of our soul. God is calling His Church to war against every demonic spirit out there. One of the things that hurts my heart is that I hear the Church saying, "If we don't mess with the devil, he won't mess with us." Thank God not all churches are speaking this lie. Most of the churches in the Western world believe this, though. When we bank on that idea, we are sleeping with the enemy. Spiritual warfare is vital in our Christian walk. There is no ceasefire because what you don't destroy in the spirit realm will end up destroying you and stealing God's best in your life. We need to move in our authority of the Holy Spirit day in and day out. One thing the enemy knows and recognizes and has to bow his knee to is the authority of Jesus Christ.

One of the most blessed Scriptures is found in Acts 19:15: "One day the evil spirit answered them, 'Jesus I know, and Paul I know about, but who are you?'" The demons understand the authority of God. We need to examine ourselves as believers and ask ourselves the million-dollar question: Do we know that we carry that authority? Does the enemy's kingdom know that about us? If not, you are no threat to it.

Many times Christians are more infatuated with silly stuff, like, can a Christian be demon possessed, when we should be more concerned about living a victorious life in Christ. It's time that the Church arise and take its rightful place on the earth. I get precious emails from many believers around the world who are being tormented by demonic forces, but it's time we put a stop to it and for us to torment them back. Let's put on the whole armor of God the right way and be the army of the Church of Jesus Christ.

We can't go around thinking that we can just put on one piece of our armor, and that we are going to defeat the enemy this way. In other words, you can't give God one piece of who you are and then let the devil own the rest. We have to be honest and genuine with ourselves and live a surrendered life to Jesus Christ. The urgency in my heart is to shed light on how the enemy infiltrates the lives of believers and trips them up to believe that it's OK to be stuck in whatever area of life that they are stuck in. Believers justify it by saying they are struggling. The truth and reality is that we haven't surrendered ourselves completely to God, and the enemy plays on that.

It's time to let go and cut the rope of those things that are hurting us spiritually. We need to know our place and what God has called us to do. Many Christians are living a life outside of God's divine purpose. It's like the generation of Moses, living and dying in the desert when God called them to do far more than that.

In the Old Testament, these precious people saw the power of God in the ten plagues, and they saw God wipe the most powerful enemy of their time off the planet. Then these people ended up in the most difficult book of the Old Testament, the Book of Numbers. A people handpicked by God started geographically on a journey that was supposed to take them eleven days, but they turned it into forty years in the wilderness. How is it that they allowed the enemy to get the best of them, by allowing the spirits of fear, unbelief, and murmuring in those forty years? Instead of them growing up, all they did was grow old. No breakthrough, no spiritual maturity, and all that time they couldn't see or hear God.

Many of us find ourselves in that same predicament. Saved for ten or twenty or thirty years but bearing no fruit, with no spiritual growth, and many don't know their purpose and destiny and why He called them into His Kingdom. Instead of bearing fruit for Jesus Christ, we have become barren fig trees: A form of religion, but denying the power. We have lost our way.

It's time to get back to the perfect will of God and move from glory to glory.

Many times we think that because we get quick victories we have defeated the devil, and we feel like we are on the mountaintop. It's like King David when he killed Goliath in a matter of minutes, but that wasn't his real spiritual warfare event. His real spiritual warfare was the preparation that God was putting him through—running away from Saul for thirteen years before he became king.

I believe that all these demonic activities that are taking place against the Body of Christ are a preparation—to bring us out to live a life in Christ of spiritual warfare. My emphasis for every brother, sister, and leader is for them to make lifestyle choices to please God. This spiritual warfare chapter is to prepare you and equip you to stand against the enemy's kingdom at any given time and to know your purpose in Jesus Christ so you won't die prematurely, outside of the will of God.

Many of us ask ourselves the ultimate question: how is it that a sovereign God is watching over me, yet I could die prematurely? Simple: By the choices we make, allowing the devil to get his ways. The devil is pushing us to make bad decisions to take us off course from the purpose and destiny God has created for us, by pushing us to bypass our prayer closet.

The Bible says we should pray without ceasing and wait on God until He responds. But too often we start making desperate decisions that can cost us many setbacks, or even a lifetime of setbacks. One of the greatest tricks the devil pushes on us is to get us to make a permanent decision based on a temporary situation, especially when we are going through trials, testings, or storms. We compartmentalize the situation of the attack.

Let me share an example. We might start to say, "this is a good day," "this is a bad day," or "this is a good week" or a bad week. Even in our workplaces, one day we say "this is a good job" and the next day we say "this is a bad job." When we start seeing things in parts, then the devil is having a field day, since we are on a spiritual roller coaster with no balance, and we allow the enemy to put on us a spirit of discontentment, when the Word of the Lord makes it clear, in 1 Timothy 6:6, that "godliness with contentment is great gain."

There is a great promise in the Word of God. God works out the good and the bad for those who love Him. "And we know that in all things God works for the good of those who love Him, who have been called according to His purpose" (Rom. 8:28 NIV). Jesus knows the beginning from the end of your life. Let us stop making it easy for the enemy to have his way in our lives.

Another error we make is that we focus too much on the circumstance and situation. We sit and ponder it, and that gives the devil great power to crush us in our circumstance. Instead of us just looking at or glancing at it, and then focusing on the solution that God already has promised us to come out of it. We need to stop spending too much time in the ashes of the circumstances, so the enemy won't get the best of us in the season we find ourselves in.

Always know that whatever you're going through, God has already signed off on it because He is trusting you to trust Him to bring you out. The Church needs to come back to prayer, not to programs or projects or building bigger church buildings while the devil laughs out loud. The early Church never built a house of God on programs and projects. It was through prayer and fasting and the Word of God.

Many of the churches in America, I am very careful to say this, their focus is distorted and the true vision of the Church—to set people free from the grips of Satan and bring them to Christ—has been taken away. Very few churches have spiritual warfare training; most have no intercessory prayer team and no deliverance ministry. People come to church sick and go back home in the same condition because their church wants to live in the modern world of entertainment, with no backbone. That's not the Church of Jesus Christ. I plead with the Church today to get back to the blueprint of the early Church to cast out demons, heal the sick, baptize the people, and bring the people into salvation and discipleship. This is the true Church of Jesus Christ.

I am not judging the Church. Only God has the right to judge His Church. I say these words with a tender heart. I am calling the Church to come to life and be the end-time Church of Jesus Christ on earth. It's engraved in my heart to call the Church to the place of supreme authority in the Lord to set the captives free.

Spiritual Warfare Weaponry

Spiritual warfare is a must; trust me, I know. We need to wake up, beloved, and be the Church with the authority that Jesus Christ has placed on us to destroy the works of darkness. We are sons and daughters of the most high God—what a God we serve. Let me leave you with the most lethal supernatural weapons that every believer is armed with.

Weapon #1: **The name of Jesus** – but not in a superstitious way. I mean brandish the name of Jesus with the power of the Holy Spirit. You're claiming the supremacy of God's sovereignty and authority in the face of every demon that shows up to fight.

Weapon #2: **The Word of God** and proclaiming the supremacy of God's Word. "For the word of God is living and powerful, and sharper than any two-edged sword" (Heb. 4:12 NKJV). Jesus Christ illustrated this in the wilderness when He destroyed the devil with the Word of God.

Weapon #3: **The blood of Jesus** and proclaiming the victory of the Cross. Revelation 12:11 says: "And they overcame him by [the power of] the blood of the lamb…" (NKJV).

Weapon #4: **The word of our testimony**; this speaks about who we are in Christ, our identity of who we are in Christ. Again, declaring the victory of the Cross, Revelation 12:11 says: "They overcame…by the word of their testimony…" (NKJV).

Weapon #5: **An obedient life.** Fear comes over the kingdom of Satan when we live an obedient life. It brings the devil to his knees. The devil can only operate and succeed with his attack when we step out of that obedient life.

Weapon #6: **Praise and worship** is when we proclaim the supremacy of our God and who He is. Psalm 150:6 says, "Let everything that has breath praise the Lord" (NKJV). Praise turns the devil's kingdom upside down.

Weapon #7: **Our heavenly language.** Speaking in tongues builds up our inner man when we are in communion with our God. In the Scriptures, Paul makes a profound statement by saying, "I speak in tongues more than all of you" (1 Cor. 14:18 NIV). Paul is sharing the importance and power we have in Christ when we speak in tongues.

Weapon #8: A **life of prayer** defeats the enemy of your soul and gives you a direct connection to the One who created you, God, and it builds your relationship with Jesus Christ.

Weapon #9: **Finding your purpose** and destiny that God has designed for you to walk in so you can destroy the works of darkness. This produces fruit for the Kingdom of Jesus Christ.

Weapon #10: **Fasting** is so important. Many people fasted in the Bible. Fasting moves the heart of God and brings breakthrough in the spiritual realm. In the days of old it saved nations, won battles and wars, destroyed strongholds, and brought the devil to his knees

Weapon #11: **Intercessory prayer** destroys and dismantles the devil's kingdom in the spirit realm. In the Bible, brothers like Daniel and Nehemiah and sisters like Esther, along with many others, interceded for others and got the victory.

Weapon #12: We must have **perseverance**, and with the authority and confidence we have in Jesus Christ. We have to be more determined and more consistent than the enemy. Perseverance is not an occasional thing; it's a commitment and a lifestyle to the supremacy of our Lord and Savior Jesus Christ, walking in His power in faith, knowing who He is and who we are in Him.

Summary

These are our supernatural weapons against the enemy—any principalities, demons, witchcraft, voodoo, and generational curses. If Christ is with us, who can stand against us? (see Rom. 8:31). We are the army of Jesus Christ. Have no mercy on the devil and his plan against your life. Never give up, and know that Jesus Christ knows where you are at all times. Many times we make spiritual warfare mystical, difficult, or even challenging, but God has made it simple for us to get the victory all the time.

CHAPTER
NINE

Red Alert for Warfare

Inside the Mind of an Ex-Devil Worshiper

In the twenty-five years I served the dark side, we had a strategy and militant game plan to take over neighborhoods and regions, because if you can take over these territories you can paralyze the churches in the spirit realm. Most of our work was done during the night, when Christians were sleeping. I am compelled to write this chapter because I feel called to be a watchman on the wall to bring an alertness to the Church. It's time to wake up and take over what the devil has stolen from us: Our neighborhoods, our communities, even the very state or country you live in. We need to take back these regions from the diabolical witches and warlocks that are operating under the radar.

Let me give you an example of how they infiltrate and take over geographical areas that they take over first in the spirit realm; because everything starts in the spirit realm before you see it manifest in the natural.

For example, the riots that started in New York City over racial unrest, spread from New York to Ferguson, Missouri, and then it went down to Baltimore. These are demonic forces that are being transferred from one region to another. These are patterns and cycles of the devil.

How we combat this in the spirit realm as believers is, as soon as we see something like this manifest, we dismantle it through prayer and fasting in the spirit realm so it will not carry over to other locations that will affect our generation. We need to curse it, cut it, and uproot it—and that's how we accomplish through Christ Jesus and the Holy Spirit to defeat the enemy and his game plan.

As a demonic high priest, at night I would leave my body and fly over neighborhoods, hurling taunts and curses down on the people who lived within their borders. Caught in the grip of strange dreams, I would feel myself being transported into different neighborhoods within the five boroughs of New York City. These out-of-body experiences (called *astral projection*) allowed me to have dominion over the communities. I felt diabolical, like a vampire, and I knew they had nothing on me. Sometimes I would even land and walk around the neighborhoods, bringing curses, bad luck, and the witchcraft aura.

Oddly, however, in some neighborhoods I met with strong resistance and at first couldn't understand where the opposing power came from. In these neighborhoods, people were waiting for me to land. I prepared to curse the neighborhood, but when I landed a mob would chase me for blocks and I couldn't curse them. Frustrated, I would fly off again, hovering as high as the streetlamps, and they would look up at me. Finally I realized these were the nasty Christians praying for their neighborhoods, their communities, their families—the prayers of the people I hated the most. Wherever these praying Christians lived, I couldn't penetrate the neighborhood. I got in, but I couldn't do the evil acts I had come to perform. So I would move on to the next neighborhood.

There are some strategic things believers can do, at strategic *times* and *places*, to destroy the works of the devil. Let's take a look at some of them in this next section.

Believers' Marching Orders

In the first week of December, the witches and warlocks are preparing themselves to usher out principalities and powers to another region and bring in new ones. Sometimes you see a drastic change in the neighborhood or region, with a dramatic shift from one demonic situation to another. They keep things fresh this way, and keep things on the move, so they can stay one step ahead of the Church. The kingdom of darkness always wants to be one step ahead of the Church because it wants to be in control. As an ex-devil worshiper, I attended these meetings.

"And from the time John the Baptist began preaching until now, the Kingdom of Heaven has been forcefully advancing, and violent people are attacking it" (Matt. 11:12 NLT). It goes without saying that all believers should pray at all times, but for a targeted approach, I recommend the following. In early December, instead of going to the mall and thinking about buying gifts, we should be armed and ready spiritually to destroy the works of the devil. We should be armed and ready—through both corporate prayer and in the personal prayer closet—to destroy the enemy's plans, "so that no advantage would be taken of us by Satan, for we are not ignorant of his schemes" (2 Cor. 2:11 NASB).

Halloween: A Demonic Masquerade

Halloween and November 1st are when the strongest attacks come out of the enemy's camps—Halloween because it's the devil's holiday, and November 1st because it's called All Saints' Day, but the reality is that it's All Demons' Day. While they make you think you're celebrating dead relatives, preparing meals and food, and paying your respects at the cemeteries, the reality is that you're doing it all to demons. For twenty-five years, those were my practices.

Regarding Halloween, I believe the Church should rise up and do night vigils to destroy the witchcraft and diabolical rituals that go on throughout the night. These rituals are aimed toward the Church, to weaken us in the Spirit. So we need to stop celebrating "Harvest" and dressing up in costumes as biblical characters—that's just trying to Christianize Halloween by putting Jesus' name on it, which is not even biblical. Instead, we must be armed and fighting spiritually for our neighborhoods and those who don't know Jesus.

Reclaiming the Four Corners

As a practicing warlock, I used to do an unusual thing—something that most people outside of the demonic world have never heard of. It's called *locking down the corners* of a neighborhood. This practice needs to be exposed. First, let me explain what this means.

Twice a year, my fellow high-ranked devil worshipers and I would go into the neighborhoods the devil assigned us to, past midnight, and stand at an intersection and do a blood ritual to conquer that territory. We called it *possessing the land*, because the four corners represent the north, the south, the east, and the west, and also the crossroads of the world or the crossroads of someone's life. At the beginning of the year we locked it down, and in the middle of the year we reinforced the ritual.

There are two reasons why we did this: 1) if you went into a witchcraft fight with a high-ranking witch, or anyone in the witchcraft world, you already had the upper hand over the person you opposed because you already conquered that territory, so they couldn't put witchcraft on it; 2) that's how the principalities of that region, from the first and second heavens, operate—through those gateways and portals; 3) if you wanted to do witchcraft against someone, you had already locked down the person's crossroads, or his life, his community, or his travels, so you could destroy the person three ways—so if you moved to Europe, I'd still got you.

As believers today, we need to tear down these strongholds and the spiritual, Satanic wars that have been unleashed in our neighborhoods. How do we do this? I recommend that Christians go to main intersections or areas of our communities and pray and break those rituals. You would see a change in the atmosphere in your communities.

I have a friend who is a pastor and apostle in Orlando, Florida, and after I shared this knowledge with him from my past, he was led by the Holy Spirit to go out to a major intersection in the city and destroy the strongholds that had been put up by the witches and warlocks in his area.

As a believer matures in the faith, he or she should develop spiritual discernment and learn how to be led by the Holy Spirit and be sensitive to His promptings. I suggest you ask the Lord in prayer, "Heavenly Father, in the name of Jesus Christ, show me and take me to the strongholds of my city. As the walls of Jericho went down, so will these strongholds come down. Let it be so, in Jesus' name."

Reversing a Curse in Germany

In 2013, a dynamic church in Nuremburg, Germany, invited me to come preach and bring down the demonic strongholds in their city. I'm not sure if you're aware of this, but Germany—the country that gave us Martin Luther and the Gutenberg Bible—is now so atheistic and post-Christian that you can feel the coldness and the chill in the atmosphere. In the 1930s, the churches of Germany got together and (in effect) asked the Holy Spirit to leave, saying they didn't want His divine presence to be part of their churches anymore. This tragic decision gave the devil the opportunity to usher in Hitler and his death regime—murdering six million Jews and over three thousand evangelical Christians who stood with them.

During my evangelistic visit to Germany, the spiritual warfare started as soon as the plane landed. The atmosphere was so heavy I was surprised that the plane landed well. The driver that was supposed to pick us up never showed up because the devil had dislocated his back. We had to sit in the airport for eight hours before someone was able to pick us up. It seemed the devil wanted to wear us out physically so we couldn't operate spiritually.

We weren't about to give in to his devices—not for a moment. We came to fight. Already pushing through horrible insomnia and headaches, things got even worse when I felt something pierce through my lung, and for the rest of the trip I had serious breathing issues. In spite of all this warfare, the Word went out and people got saved and delivered from demonic bondages, including from rape and child molestation. One family had not even spoken to each other in twelve years, but they all came together in forgiveness and the healing power of Jesus Christ.

On the last day of the trip, before I came home, the hosting pastors asked us to go pray with them on a particular mountain—the highest point in Germany—from which Hitler and his generals cursed the entire nation. I thought this was going to be a little mountain; they never described it to me. (In New York, we've got small mountains.) So we took a two-hour train ride to the location, then a trolley up the mountain for twenty minutes. When we got off the trolley I thought that was the place. There was snow up there and you could see for miles around. I started to pray, but to my surprise they said, "Not yet;...we're not there yet."

I said, "What do you mean we're not there yet? This is the top of the mountain, right?" They shook their heads and pointed up higher.

We had to take this tram suspended from cables up to the highest part of the peak—I've never seen anything like that in my life. I was shocked and dismayed. Fear gripped me so fast that I didn't even have a chance to say "ouch." This little cart disappeared into the clouds, and the earth disappeared underneath me. Instead of the warfare prayer, I started praying the sinner's prayer!

When it landed, we got out and were led to a platform. We were so high up that you could see Austria right next door. We wrote a declaration for Germany, reclaiming it for God and inviting the Holy Spirit back—and breaking every demonic curse that was declared in the airwaves from Hitler on up, and even in the churches. The pastor placed the declaration in a small glass bottle and threw it over the mountain, over Germany.

A week later, when I came back home, to my surprise, one of Hitler's generals who was living in the States was apprehended and brought to trial. He was ninety-five years old. Many of the families that had left the faith returned to the German pastor's house of worship. And when I got home, my lung was miraculously healed.

The Church needs to rise up over the powers of darkness. We need to attack them from our position in the third heaven— seated with Jesus Christ, higher than the highest in the heavens, the position of all authority over the kingdom of darkness—so we can take our country back. We as believers in Christ need to be living in righteousness and holiness, not being in bed with the devil or the world. Then we will have the victory.

Modern-Day Nehemiahs: Rebuilding the Walls

The reason why these demonic activities are happening is because the Church is not being the Church, praying corporately and individually, together as one in Christ.

When I used to astral-project over neighborhoods to curse them in the spirit realm, the saints in prayer would chase me out of their neighborhoods, and I was ineffective to accomplish my mission. In a spiritual sense, those praying believers were like the remnant of Israel that returned to Jerusalem with Nehemiah to rebuild the crumbling walls of the city.

The devil has brought down the spiritual walls of this country, and we as the Church need to start building up those spiritual walls like the Israelites did. What they did in the physical, we need to start doing in the spiritual. They all got together in one accord and unity, and each person decided to play a part together, building right next to each other. Scripture says they would build with one hand and hold a sword in the other hand, while the enemy—through Sanballat and Tobias—tried to discourage them and get them off their game plan so they could not accomplish the blessing of the Lord for their region.

The enemy tried to bring distraction and fear upon God's chosen people, but the devil today has accomplished not only to bring down the walls, but he also has divided the Church. Where is the remnant today that will stand, under strong leadership like Nehemiah, and say NO! to the enemy and YES! to Jesus Christ?! We need to put ourselves and our own agendas to the side and get back together, united as one in Christ. We need to stop allowing the devil to divide us with names and titles and positions. The greatest title in the Kingdom is *Servant*. It's time to pick up the towel, wrap it around our waist, and get to the battlefield.

I believe in my heart that the Church will rise again and take its position on Earth and be the Church that Jesus died for, like the Church in the book of Acts—going out to the streets and preaching the true Gospel at any cost, and setting the captives free.

Many times we talk about so many illegal immigrants crossing the border, many people, all kinds of people crossing the border, so imagine how many things are happening in the spiritual, how many things in the spirit dimension are crossing over from one region to another. We have churches all over the world. Just think what would happen if we all started to pray, one big Church, one Jesus, the real Church—what would happen to Satan and his cronies? Wow, that would be awesome, an awesome victory, how we could bring the Church to the forefront, and many would be saved and delivered out of the hands of the devil.

I remember when I was a warlock in the demon world, we used to have these meetings once a year, coming together to take over the spirit world, attacking, dismantling, and paralyzing everything that had to do with good that opposed evil. We would destroy anything that was ready to give birth (spiritually) so it would not manifest, not allow that person to fulfill their destiny. Whatever region, whatever domain, whatever city or country or community or people or church, before they reached their peak, we would kill it and cut it at the root. If the churches would realize how important the spirit world is, and how much we need each other, and there's only one Church in Jesus Christ, if we were to come together and fight the good fight against the kingdom of darkness, this would be a wakeup call to the world, and many unbelievers as well as believers. And how would God's heart feel?

Let's stop the devil from bleeding us spiritually. It's time to get together and be the Church of the living God. Instead of praying for jobs, big homes, cars, or strategies to make our church bigger—and perhaps these are good things—but I haven't seen or heard the Church challenge its members to fight in the spirit and be more than conquerors in Christ Jesus.

Faith vs. the Flesh

The Church is trying to fight a supernatural battle using their fallen-man nature, and that will never work. We also are trying to fight the devil with the "fig tree" religious system. I'll explain what I mean in just a minute. There's a Scripture that talks about "having a form of godliness, but denying the power thereof..." (see 2 Tim. 3:5).

When Adam and Eve were defeated in the Garden, they covered themselves with fig leaves because they lost their true covering with God. When we lose our true covering with God, we try to find something to replace it with, and that's a dangerous thing for any believer, because that brings a religious system tied to a religious spirit. And the devil is all over that.

It's an amazing thing in the New Testament that Jesus cursed a fig tree, because a fig tree represented the religious system of that day, but it was a system of barrenness and no fruit; there was no evidence of the hand of God upon someone's life.

In Hebrews 11, several ordinary people are listed in what's become known as the "Hall of Fame of Faith." They defeated the kingdom of darkness with just one thing: Faith in God. Normal men and women stepped into the supernatural and accomplished amazing victories.

Ephesians 6 speaks about the powers of darkness, but it also talks about the armor of God. As much as we read about the armor and try to put it on, there's one requirement: How is your faith in Christ? Are you willing to stand and guard the territory that God has given you? Territory is so important to the devil. Territory can be your family/household, your neighborhood, your career, your ministry, or even the geographical region. Territory can be both tangible and intangible ground that the enemy wants to capture for his evil purposes, because if he can capture those, he can capture the people that occupy it—or he can rob you of your purpose and destiny.

Just to prove to you that territory is so important to the devil, I will show you two incidents in the Bible. The first story, in Luke 8:26-39, takes place when Jesus and His disciples journey into the region of Gadara.

> *Then they sailed to the country of the Gerasenes, which is opposite Galilee. And when He came out onto the land, He was met by a man from the city who was possessed with demons; and who had not put on any clothing for a long time, and was not living in a house, but in the tombs. Seeing Jesus, he cried out and fell before Him, and said in a loud voice, "What business do we have with each other, Jesus, Son of the Most High God? I beg You, do not torment me." For He had commanded the unclean spirit to come out of the man. For it had seized him many times; and he was bound with chains and shackles and kept under guard, and yet he would break his bonds and be driven by the demon into the desert. And Jesus asked him, "What is your name?" And he said, "Legion"; for many demons had entered him. They were imploring Him not to command them to go away into the abyss.*

Now there was a herd of many swine feeding there on the mountain; and the demons implored Him to permit them to enter the swine. And He gave them permission. And the demons came out of the man and entered the swine; and the herd rushed down the steep bank into the lake and was drowned.

When the herdsmen saw what had happened, they ran away and reported it in the city and out in the country. The people went out to see what had happened; and they came to Jesus, and found the man from whom the demons had gone out, sitting down at the feet of Jesus, clothed and in his right mind; and they became frightened. Those who had seen it reported to them how the man who was demon-possessed had been made well. And all the people of the country of the Gerasenes and the surrounding district asked Him to leave them, for they were gripped with great fear; and He got into a boat and returned. But the man from whom the demons had gone out was begging Him that he might accompany Him; but He sent him away, saying, "Return to your house and describe what great things God has done for you." So he went away, proclaiming throughout the whole city what great things Jesus had done for him (Luke 8:26-39 NASB).

As you can see from the story, the demons didn't really care whether they were in the man or the pigs. They knew that if they lost the territory that was assigned to them, they would lose rank, authority, and their mission from Satan. So they begged Jesus not to send them out of the region.

The second incident occurs in the Old Testament in the Book of First Samuel, when Jonathan and his armor bearer crept into the Philistines' camp and took away a hundred feet of territory from them, and it shook them to the core. Israel was able to win the victory that day. In this story, the armor bearer symbolically represents the Holy Spirit. You can read the story for yourself in First Samuel 14:13-15.

> *Then Jonathan climbed up on his hands and feet, with his armor bearer behind him; and they fell before Jonathan, and his armor bearer put some to death after him. That first slaughter which Jonathan and his armor bearer made was about twenty men within about half a furrow in an acre of land. And there was a trembling in the camp, in the field, and among all the people. Even the garrison and the raiders trembled, and the earth quaked so that it became a great trembling* (NASB).

The Revelation

The book of Revelation tells how we believers are coming into a rest on the earth that lasts a thousand years. It's one of God's amazing promises. But for now, there's a kingdom of darkness, commandeered by the devil, that carries *his* promises. The Bible speaks about the kingdom of the enemy being here, now, on the earth. The Word of the Lord goes on to say that Satan is the god of this world, but there's no future in his kingdom. There's no tomorrow, no hope, no real benefits—only temporary fixes and pleasures. However, they come at a cost: your soul.

Jesus Christ has established His kingdom on this earth as well, which is the Church. There is also a heavenly Kingdom, and the millennial Kingdom on the earth. Revelation chapter 20 speaks about the Kingdom that will reign for one thousand years of peace on the earth. Spiritual warfare will cease. That blows my mind. Let me shed some light on this amazing event, which involves the removal of the devil himself, the removal of pure evil.

> *Then I saw an angel coming down from heaven, holding the key of the abyss and a great chain in his hand. And he laid hold of the dragon, the serpent of old, who is the devil and Satan, and bound him for a thousand years; and he threw him into the abyss, and shut it and sealed it over him, so that he would not deceive the nations any longer, until the thousand years were completed; after these things he must be released for a short time* (Rev. 20:1-3 NASB).

So how is it that many churches today are preaching that we should not have any worries about Satan? Saying things like, "He can't do anything to us," or "He's no threat to the Church" or "We don't have to engage in spiritual warfare anymore." But the Word of God is clear, and it tells us in First Peter 5:8 (NLT): "Stay alert! Watch out for your great enemy, the devil. He prowls around like a roaring lion, looking for someone to devour."

Believers, especially leaders, are saying that the kingdom of darkness is defeated. But John 10:10 says that the devil comes to steal, kill, and destroy. Many precious saints are walking around spiritually sick, defeated, bound with generational curses, with open doors to the devil, and the devil has legal rights over many of God's people.

Who is willing to step into the gap and stop the spiritual bleeding that is going on in the Body of Christ today? We are blinded and have no spiritual vision, no discernment, and are no longer concerned about the things that are going on in the spirit realm. The Bible says, in Hosea 4:6 (NLT): "My people are being destroyed because they don't know Me. Since you priests [religious leaders] refuse to know Me, I refuse to recognize you as my priests. Since you have forgotten the laws of your God, I will forget to bless your children."

Special Ops within the Church

With the onslaught of demonic attacks, there's an urgent call on the true Church of Jesus Christ today. It's time to wake up and stop playing patty-cake with the devil. We are called to destroy the works of darkness now. And if you ask me how we do that, I'm glad you asked. I believe in my heart that the Church should be armed and dangerous by having

- Spiritual Warfare ministries,

- Intercessory ministries, and

- Deliverance ministries.

These are super-powerful ministries, and I will break down all three and explain the differences between them. We need these ministries for the times we're in and for the coming days.

The first team, the elite "Special Ops" spiritual warfare team, should engage the enemy head-on, going into the devil's camp with the power of the Holy Spirit, destroying every opposition, stronghold, and weapon that he has against us. Their prayers should be focused on spiritual territories—territories in the local communities, cities, states, regions, and nations.

The second elite team, the intercessory ministry, has a mission to intercede for pastors and leaders, families, and the unsaved; and not only for their church, but for all the churches around the world and for the nations. This will change things in the spiritual atmosphere.

The third elite team, the deliverance ministry, should perform deliverance once a week on believers who are bound through generational curses or open doors to the enemy: tearing down strongholds, breaking legal rights, uprooting curses, and closing doors on the enemy's face.

When we apply these ministries, the devil and his losers—fallen angels—don't stand a chance in hell against the Church of Jesus Christ.

Finally, let me share a revelation I got from the Lord on the importance of fighting back. If we start doing these things, we will see the victory of the Cross 100 percent. We have to reinforce that victory in the face of evil. Let's put the devil on notice. He picked the wrong house, he picked the wrong church, he picked the wrong family to mess with. But we are more determined than he is. Amen.

I would like to point out something quickly. As I mentioned above, Revelation 20:1-3 talks about the removal of the devil. Sweet; I love it!

> *Then I saw an angel coming down from heaven, holding the key of the abyss and a great chain in his hand. And he laid hold of the dragon, the serpent of old, who is the devil and Satan, and bound him for a thousand years; and he threw him into the abyss,*

and shut it and sealed it over him, so that he would not deceive the nations any longer, until the thousand years were completed; after these things he must be released for a short time (Rev. 20:1-3 NASB).

I love this part; I'll paraphrase it for you. The angel came down, grabbed the devil by the throat, threw him down into the pit, and chained him up. Please listen to this: He didn't come down with white gloves, like the Church is trying to fight the devil today. The angel threw him down because the devil is a nobody. This event is going to supernaturally change the world because Satan is supposed to be the prince of this world, or the god of this age; he's the god of the children of disobedience. He's the master of every occult group. This should be a wakeup call to all in the political world, the music world, and the entertainment world. Your time is short, just like your daddy's.

My prayers go out for all. It's time to open up your eyes and bend your knees to Jesus Christ. I say this for the sake of saving your soul-man. I've been to hell, and I don't recommend it. I want to say that those who put their faith in Christ: Don't be deceived into thinking there's no spiritual battle taking place. Let's stop the lies about "we don't need to fight anymore against the kingdom of darkness."

Summary

Again, Revelation 20 tells it all. We have a war on our hands through the power of the Holy Spirit to defeat and destroy anything spiritual that opposes the Kingdom of our God. That is the mission that Jesus left on the earth for the Church to accomplish: To set the captives free.

CHAPTER

TEN

A Guide to Spiritual Freedom

We've covered a lot of ground in this book, and as we come to the conclusion, I'd like to give you a practical guide for getting free and *staying* free of demonic strongholds and the devil's arsenal of weapons. We've touched on some of these topics in other parts of the book, but I wanted to gather the nine critical components of spiritual warfare in one place—especially for readers who may pick up this book and turn straight to this chapter.

As we go into the enemy's camp with the following material, remember this verse: "For I can do everything through Christ, who gives me strength" (Phil. 4:13 NLT).

Here are the nine critical areas in spiritual warfare you need to know:

1. War Has Been Declared on Mankind

2. The Origin of Satan—Fallen Angels and Demons

3. Mark 16: The Assignment of Every Believer

4. Can a Christian Have a Demon?

5. Ways Demons Gain Access

6. Our Authority Over Demons

7. Binding and Loosing—The Keys to the Kingdom

8. How to Cast Out Devils

9. Generational Curses and How to Break Them

Before we dive in, let me ask you a very important question:

Do you know Jesus Christ as Lord?

If you have been reading this book and have never made a decision to ask Jesus Christ into your heart, now is the time to make your decision and have your name added to the Lamb's Book of Life.

As Jesus taught the crowds about the Kingdom of God, one day He cast a demon out of a man who couldn't speak. The second that demon left him, the man could speak again— and of course the people were amazed and started asking Jesus how He did it. Jesus said something profound that is key to spiritual deliverance.

When an evil spirit leaves a person, it goes into the desert, searching for rest. But when it finds none, it says, 'I will return to the person I came from.' So it returns and finds that its former home is all swept and in order. Then the spirit finds seven other spirits more evil than itself, and they all enter the person and live there. And so that person is worse off than before (Luke 11:24-26 NLT).

I don't take deliverance lightly, and, for that reason, I won't pray a prayer of deliverance over someone who is not born again by the Holy Spirit. An unbeliever who gets delivered of a demonic spirit (or spirits) does not have the indwelling Holy Spirit to "fill his house"—it's been swept clean, but as Jesus taught, that demon will go find seven other demons and return to have a party, and that person will be worse off than if he never got delivered at all.

If you believe you are being tormented by demons, but you have never made Jesus Christ the Lord of your life, please read through the Scriptures below and finish with the Sinner's Prayer. As you do, you will be born into the Kingdom of God and washed by the blood that Jesus shed on Calvary.

Here is what the Bible declares:

1. We are all sinners and cannot save ourselves.

For all have sinned, and come short of the glory of God (Rom. 3:23).

Not by works of righteousness which we have done, but according to His mercy He saved us, by the washing of regeneration, and renewing of the Holy Ghost (Titus 3:5).

How shall we escape, if we neglect so great salvation; which at the first began to be spoken by the Lord, and was confirmed unto us by them that heard Him (Heb. 2:3).

For by grace are ye saved through faith; and that not of yourselves: it is the gift of God: Not of works, lest any man should boast (Eph. 2:8-9).

2. We must confess our sins and repent of them, which means to forsake them.

If we confess our sins, He is faithful and just to forgive us our sins, and to cleanse us from all unrighteousness (1 John 1:9).

He that covereth his sins shall not prosper: but whoso confesseth and forsaketh them shall have mercy (Prov. 28:13).

3. Jesus Christ is the only way of salvation.

For God so loved the world, that He gave His only begotten Son, that whosoever believeth in Him should not perish, but have everlasting life (John 3:16).

He that believeth on the Son hath everlasting life: and he that believeth not the Son shall not see life; but the wrath of God abideth on him (John 3:36).

Jesus saith unto him, I am the way, the truth, and the life: no man cometh unto the Father, but by Me (John 14:6).

For Christ also hath once suffered for sins, the just for the unjust, that He might bring us to God, being put to death in the flesh, but quickened by the Spirit... (1 Pet. 3:18).

Be it known unto you all, and to all the people of Israel, that by the name of Jesus Christ of Nazareth, whom ye crucified, whom God raised from the dead, even by Him doth this man stand here before you whole. This is the stone which was set at nought of you builders, which is become the head of the corner. Neither is there salvation in any other: for there is none other name under heaven given among men, whereby we must be saved (Acts 4:10-12).

...That if you confess with your mouth Jesus as Lord, and believe in your heart that God raised Him from the dead, you will be saved; for with the heart a person believes, resulting in righteousness, and with the mouth he confesses, resulting in salvation. For the Scripture says, "whoever believes in Him will not be disappointed." For there is no distinction between Jew and Greek; for the same Lord is Lord of all, abounding in riches for all who call on Him; for "whoever will call on the name of the lord will be saved" (Rom. 10:9-13 NASB).

For by grace are ye saved through faith; and that not of yourselves: it is the gift of God: Not of works, lest any man should boast. For we are his workmanship, created in Christ Jesus unto good works, which God hath before ordained that we should walk in them (Eph. 2:8-10).

The Bible teaches us that deliverance is the "children's bread" (see Matt. 15:22-28), and so if you do not know Jesus Christ as Lord and Savior, I want you to pray this prayer right now with me.

> *"Father God, in Jesus Christ's name I come to You today and I confess that I am a sinner."*
>
> *"I confess with my mouth that Jesus Christ is Lord and I believe in my heart that Jesus Christ died on the Cross for my sins, and that He rose again on the third day and is now seated at the right hand of God the Father and will return one day for me."*
>
> *"I now confess all my sins known and unknown, and repent of them."*
>
> *"Lord Jesus Christ, I ask You to forgive me and cleanse me from all sin."*
>
> *"Lord Jesus Christ, I ask You to come into my heart and be my Lord and Savior and to fill me with Your Holy Spirit."*
>
> *"Thank You, Lord Jesus Christ, for saving me with Your precious blood."*

If you just prayed that prayer, *you are now born again.* Welcome to the family of God!

Nine Critical Areas in Spiritual Warfare

1. *War Has Been Declared on Mankind*

Satan and his fallen angels and the demonic hordes of unclean spirits hate mankind. They want to see you and me dead because we were created in the image of God.

There is no plan of salvation for Satan and his fallen angels and demons, and for this reason they hate you and me with a passion, knowing they are doomed to the Lake of Fire, and they want to take as many human souls with them as they can before their time is up.

> *Be sober, be vigilant; because your adversary the devil, as a roaring lion, walketh about, seeking whom he may devour: Whom resist steadfast in the faith, knowing that the same afflictions are accomplished in your brethren that are in the world* (1 Pet. 5:8-9).

> *The thief cometh not, but for to steal, and to kill, and to destroy: I am come that they might have life, and that they might have it more abundantly* (John 10:10).

We are fighting a real enemy who is a thief and a murderer and a destroyer, and having killed before, he now wants to kill you and me if he can. So we must learn to fight back in Jesus Christ's name if we want to survive.

If the devil can destroy you or me, you better believe he will then go after our families to do the same, and so we must fight back so we can live and stand in the gap for our loved ones, whom Satan has also targeted.

Let's look now a little more at who we are fighting and the makeup of Satan's army. I would categorize the makeup of the enemy into three areas:

Satan—He is the leader of the hosts of hell.

Fallen Angels—These spirit beings work for Satan and rule over geographical regions and locales and carry out his plans.

Unclean Spirits, also known as *Demons*—These are the foot soldiers, and they report to the fallen angels and Satan himself, and do their bidding.

> *For we wrestle not against flesh and blood, but against principalities, against powers, against the rulers of the darkness of this world, against spiritual wickedness in high places* (Eph. 6:12).

Satan commands an army that is set up like any modern-day military organization, with ranking and positions of authority. That army is comprised of fallen angels and unclean demon spirits. These hold different ranks and positions and control geographical locations, including countries, states, cities, and other locales. They carry out their orders to control and manipulate and destroy mankind.

2. *The Origin of Satan—Fallen Angels and Demons*

> *For by Him were all things created, that are in Heaven, and that are in earth, visible and invisible, whether they be thrones, or dominions, or principalities, or powers: all things were created by Him, and for Him: And He is before all things, and by Him all things consist* (Col. 1:16-17).

From the Word of God, we see that God created everything. This includes Satan (who was an anointed *cherub)* and various classes of angels: *warrior angels* (such as the archangel Michael), *messenger angels* (such as Gabriel), *seraphim, cherubim,* as well as a class of spirit beings that we know today as *demons*.

Some of the creation rebelled and followed Satan, who fell because of pride and who convinced one-third of the angels to follow him in rebellion against God.

The fallen angels were cast out of the third heaven, but they can still operate in the first and second heavens and also move in and out of planet Earth, where we live. I believe that what many people are sighting and calling UFOs are actually angels: either angels of God or fallen angels.

So we have the fallen angels who work in the heavenlies and on earth, taking orders from their leader Satan, and then the legions of unclean spirits (AKA demons) who work under the command of the fallen angels. These foot soldiers, or ground level demons, operate to gain access into people and their lives in order to control and destroy them.

Many people have speculated on the origin of demons, but we are not told much about them in the Bible, other than that they are spirits and have personalities and intellects but no physical body. This is why they roam dry places looking for rest, and why they seek out bodies they can enter into so they can physically express themselves and their wicked desires.

Demons have the ability to actually enter into and live in people, like a parasite that lives inside of its host, and they must be rooted out and kicked out in Jesus Christ's name before they are able to complete their mission, which is to kill, steal, and destroy you and me.

The good news is that, if you are a Christian, the demons cannot get into your spirit as that is sealed by the Holy Spirit, but they can inhabit your flesh and live and operate in your soul (the mind, will, and emotions) and put pressure on your mind and emotions, until they are cast out in Jesus's name.

When we become followers of Jesus, God puts a natural hedge of protection around our minds, but when we commit sin and do not repent, we break the hedge and open the door to demons. Then the viper bites us—demons can come in and set up housekeeping. "He that diggeth a pit shall fall into it; and whoso breaketh an hedge, a serpent shall bite him" (Eccles. 10:8).

Jesus Christ, the Son of God, died for you and me so that we might have eternal life by receiving Him as our Lord and Savior and following Him. As for Satan, many people picture him with a pitchfork and calling the shots from a boardroom table in hell, but hell is the last place Satan wants to be or is at this moment.

> *Now there was a day when the sons of God came to present themselves before the Lord, and Satan came also among them. And the Lord said unto Satan, Whence comest thou? Then Satan answered the Lord, and said, From going to and fro in the earth, and from walking up and down in it* (Job 1:6-7).

From the Word of God we can see that although Satan lost his position as the anointed cherub, He has not been stripped of all his power or mobility, and he is able to move in the heavenlies and also roam the earth.

> *And I heard a loud voice saying in heaven, "Now is come salvation, and strength, and the Kingdom of our God, and the power of His Christ: for the accuser*

of our brethren is cast down, which accused them before our God day and night" (Rev. 12:10).

Although Satan accuses you and me day and night, Jesus Christ—who sits at the right hand of the Father—makes intercession for us. He is our advocate with God the Father, and He defends all believers from Satan's accusations.

My little children, these things write I unto you, that ye sin not. And if any man sin, we have an advocate with the Father, Jesus Christ the righteous: And He is the propitiation for our sins: and not for ours only, but also for the sins of the whole world. And hereby we do know that we know Him, if we keep His commandments. He that saith, I know Him, and keepeth not His commandments, is a liar, and the truth is not in him. But whoso keepeth His word, in him verily is the love... (1 John 2:1-5).

The Word of God is very clear that we are born into a battle zone, and until we die and go home to meet Jesus or He returns at the Last Trumpet, we are called to be soldiers; We have a job to do, which is outlined in Mark 16 and other Scriptures.

Thou therefore, my son, be strong in the grace that is in Christ Jesus. And the things that thou hast heard of me among many witnesses, the same commit thou to faithful men, who shall be able to teach others also. Thou therefore endure hardness, as a good soldier of Jesus Christ. No man that warreth entangleth himself with the affairs of this life; that he may please Him who hath chosen him to be a soldier (2 Tim. 2:1-4).

3. *Mark 16: The Assignment of Every Believer*

And He said unto them, Go ye into all the world, and preach the gospel to every creature. He that believeth and is baptized shall be saved; but he that believeth not shall be damned. And these signs shall follow them that believe; In My name shall they cast out devils; they shall speak with new tongues; They shall take up serpents; and if they drink any deadly thing, it shall not hurt them; they shall lay hands on the sick, and they shall recover. So then after the Lord had spoken unto them, He was received up into heaven, and sat on the right hand of God. And they went forth, and preached everywhere, the Lord working with them, and confirming the word with signs following. Amen (Mark 16:15-20).

Let's look at some parallel passages in the Word of God that speak to our instructions as Christians.

Then He called His twelve disciples together, and gave them power and authority over all devils, and to cure diseases. And He sent them to preach the Kingdom of God, and to heal the sick (Luke 9:1-2).

And Jesus said unto him, No man, having put his hand to the plough, and looking back, is fit for the Kingdom of God (Luke 9:62).

The same day there came certain of the Pharisees, saying unto Him, Get thee out, and depart hence: for Herod will kill Thee. And He said unto them, Go ye, and tell that fox, Behold, I cast out devils, and I do cures to day and tomorrow, and the third day I shall be perfected (Luke 13:31-32).

And as ye go, preach, saying, The Kingdom of Heaven is at hand. Heal the sick, cleanse the lepers, raise the dead, cast out devils: freely ye have received, freely give (Matt. 10:7-8).

Then said Jesus unto His disciples, If any man will come after Me, let him deny himself, and take up his cross, and follow Me. For whosoever will save his life shall lose it: and whosoever will lose his life for My sake shall find it (Matt. 16:24-25).

And Jesus came and spake unto them, saying, All power is given unto Me in Heaven and in earth. Go ye therefore, and teach all nations, baptizing them in the name of the Father, and of the Son, and of the Holy Ghost: Teaching them to observe all things whatsoever I have commanded you: and, lo, I am with you alway, even unto the end of the world. Amen (Matt. 28:18-20).

The Curse of Meroz—For Not Fighting for the Lord

Curse ye Meroz, said the angel of the Lord, curse ye bitterly the inhabitants thereof; because they came not to the help of the Lord, to the help of the Lord against the mighty (Judg. 5:23).

To summarize, as Christians we are called to preach the Gospel, which means to tell people about Jesus Christ and His plan of salvation, and we are to be engaged in ministry with signs following, which includes casting out devils, praying for the sick, raising the dead, and moving in the power gifts of the Holy Spirit.

4. *Can a Christian Have a Demon?*

One-third of Jesus Christ's ministry dealt with casting out unclean spirits (demons), but many Christians and churches have nothing to do with the deliverance ministry—they mistakenly think that they are immune to demonic attack. They have been told by their pastors and fellow believers that demons are nothing to worry about, since a Christian cannot have a demon.

What is the truth? Can a Christian have a demon? The quick and simple answer is Yes; a Christian can have anything they open the door to.

One of the greatest lies perpetrated within the Body of Christ is that a Christian cannot have a demon, and because of this false teaching (that the Word of God does not support), deliverance and spiritual warfare are not being taught in most churches. People are being destroyed for a lack of knowledge concerning one-third of Jesus's ministry, which was the ministry of deliverance—the casting out of devils in Jesus's name.

The result is that most Christians are not equipped to deal with the attacks that Satan and his demons are launching on the family. Look at the divorce rate across the land and in the Church, and the number of broken homes. Look at how many people are battling depression and suicidal thoughts, turning to psychotropic drugs for relief. I am talking about church people, in addition to the unsaved masses.

Look at the rising numbers of pastors and churchgoers involved in adultery, fornication, pornography, prescription drug addiction, and the list goes on.

Many of God's people are bound up and dying prematurely, and the body count is mounting daily because we are ignorant of the war we are in and who our enemy is.

We Are Made Up of Multiple Parts

Let's look for a moment at the makeup of a human being. You and I are made up of three parts:

- Our fleshly body

- Our spirit

- Our soul (mind—will—emotions)

When we come to Jesus Christ, our spirit is sealed till the day of redemption, but not our soul and fleshly body. Our body and soul are open targets for demonic infestation. The Word of God says that "sin lies at the door" (Gen. 4:7), so when we commit sin we open up the door to unclean spirits (demons) who will come in and begin their work to kill, steal, and destroy until they are dealt with and cast out.

Some Christians will try to cop out and blame everything on the flesh, but the truth of the matter is that you cannot crucify a demon or cast out the flesh. We must crucify the flesh, renew our minds through God's Word, and cast out the demons that have gained access through personal and generational open doors of sin. And we can do this and be delivered, in Jesus Christ's name. "If thou doest well, shalt thou not be accepted? and if thou doest not well, sin lieth at the door. And unto thee *shall be* his desire, and thou shalt rule over him" (Gen. 4:7).

5. Ways Demons Gain Access

Here are some ways by which demons can gain access to the body or soul—the mind, will, and emotions—of a believer.

- Unforgiveness

- Sexual Sin: fornication, adultery, homosexuality, sodomy, pornography

- Witchcraft and Occult: tarot cards, Ouija, psychics, Wicca, yoga, Reiki, acupuncture

- Psychotropic drugs, alcohol, marijuana

- Sins of our ancestors which bring generational curses

6. Our Authority Over Demons

If we are going to triumph over the enemy, we must understand that we have the ability to fight back. We have been given authority and power over the enemy, and the commission to set the captives free, in Jesus Christ's name.

A. Our Position in Christ

Even when we were dead in sins, hath quickened us together with Christ, (by grace ye are saved;) *And hath raised us up together, and made us sit together in heavenly places in Christ Jesus...* (Eph. 2:5-6).

B. Our Power to Cast Out Devils and Heal the Sick

And when He had called unto Him His twelve disciples, He gave them power against unclean spirits, to cast them out, and to heal all manner of sickness and all manner of disease (Matt. 10:1).

C. We Have Power Greater Than Any Power of the Enemy

Behold, I give unto you power to tread on serpents and scorpions, and over all the power of the enemy: and nothing shall by any means hurt you (Luke 10:19).

D. Demons are Subject to the Believer

...Rejoice not, that the spirits are subject unto you; but rather rejoice, because your names are written in Heaven (Luke 10:20).

From these Scriptures we can see that Jesus Christ has given each believer the commission and authority and power to use His name to cast out devils and heal the sick, and He expects us to do these things. He commanded it before He returned to Heaven.

E. We Have Been Given the Authority to Arrest Demons

Verily I say unto you, Whatsoever ye shall bind on earth shall be bound in Heaven: and whatsoever ye shall loose on earth shall be loosed in Heaven" (Matt. 18:18).

7. Binding and Loosing—The Keys to the Kingdom

"I will give you the keys of the Kingdom of Heaven; whatever you bind on earth will be bound in Heaven, and whatever you loose on earth will be loosed in Heaven" (Matt. 16:19 NKJV). Think of binding and loosing, and our assignment from Jesus Christ in Mark 16 to cast out devils, in the context of a police officer. A police officer is given a commission by the city to enforce the law, and the authority to arrest those who break the law and to take them into custody for trial by a judge. To enforce the commission and authority they have received, the police are given power in the form of a handgun and handcuffs, to use as needed to carry out their tasks.

Binding is to arrest demons, removing them from people whom they have hijacked and taken captive, and then remit the demons into hell's prison, where they will await final sentencing at the end of time, to be remanded into the Lake of Fire.

Loosing has a two-fold purpose: To set a person free who has been bound up by demons, and to send forth the angels of God on assignment in Jesus Christ's name.

Our job then is to arrest demons by binding them and loose people by casting demons out of them, setting them free in Jesus' name.

8. *How to Cast Out Devils*

Casting out devils is not complicated at all, but is a matter of speaking to the unclean spirit and using the authority given to you and every believer by Jesus Christ, commanding the unclean spirit to come out of the person in Jesus Christ's name and go.

Deliverance can come in different forms. *Personal deliverance* is when someone prays for you and commands the demons to come out in Jesus' name. *Self-deliverance* is when you use your authority and command the demons inside of you to come out in Jesus's name (we covered this earlier, in Chapter 7). *Mass deliverance* is when a minister does deliverance with a group of one or more people in a church or house meeting, and he commands demons to come out of many people at the same time in Jesus' name.

Demons can be called out by name or by function. Examples:

- "You spirit of depression—come out! In Jesus Christ's name."

- "You spirit of death—come out! In Jesus Christ's name."

- "You spirit that attacks them at night while they are sleeping—come out now! In Jesus Christ's name."

When the demon comes out, the best thing to do is take the demon out of circulation. You can do this by commanding it to go to where the Lord Jesus Christ wants it to go.

Deliverance can take time, and so requires patience and persistence. We need to understand that we are battling with the forces of darkness; all battles are not won in an instant or in a day. Deliverance from one or more unclean spirits can happen quickly, while other demons can put up a fight and remain a long time and take several deliverance sessions to be cast out, depending on whether or not they have legal rights to stay (through unconfessed sins).

Some demons are stronger than others and come out only by prayer and fasting. Some demons will not come out because the person seeking deliverance is unwilling to forgive others.

Some demons are locked into the person via the mechanism of a generational curse, and so the generational sins must first be addressed and the curses broken, and then the demons can be commanded to go and will in Jesus Christ's name.

We take back the land bit by bit, and I equate deliverance to a boxing match. Sometimes you will have to go several rounds, with rest breaks in between, before you land a knockout punch.

Every deliverance case is different and so the key is to stay humble, don't give up, and keep attacking the enemy in Jesus Christ's name.

9. *Generational Curses and How to Break Them*

I want to talk to you now about generational curses and how you can be set free. Let's start by looking at some Scriptures, to lay a biblical foundation so you can be set free of burdens that you and your family have been carrying around for a very long time.

There is power and freedom, healing and deliverance, and blessing in the Word of God. Look what the Lord says in the book of Exodus.

> *And God spake all these words, saying, I am the Lord thy God, which have brought thee out of the land of Egypt, out of the house of bondage. Thou shalt have no other gods before Me. Thou shalt not make unto thee any graven image, or any likeness of anything that is in Heaven above, or that is in the earth beneath, or that is in the water under the earth. Thou shalt not bow down thyself to them, nor serve them: for I the Lord thy God am a jealous God, visiting the iniquity of the fathers upon the children unto the third and fourth generation of them that hate me; and showing mercy unto thousands of them that love Me, and keep My commandments* (Exod. 20:1-6).

And the Lord passed by before him, and proclaimed, The Lord, The Lord God, merciful and gracious, longsuffering, and abundant in goodness and truth, keeping mercy for thousands, forgiving iniquity and transgression and sin, and that will by no means clear the guilty; visiting the iniquity of the fathers upon the children, and upon the children's children, unto the third and to the fourth generation. And Moses made haste, and bowed his head toward the earth, and worshipped (Exod. 34:6-8).

I am the Lord thy God, which brought thee out of the land of Egypt, from the house of bondage. Thou shalt have none other gods before Me. Thou shalt not make thee any graven image, or any likeness of any thing that is in Heaven above, or that is in the earth beneath, or that is in the waters beneath the earth: Thou shalt not bow down thyself unto them, nor serve them: for I the Lord thy God am a jealous God, visiting the iniquity of the fathers upon the children unto the third and fourth generation of them that hate Me, and shewing mercy unto thousands of them that love Me and keep My commandments (Deut. 5:6-10).

A bastard shall not enter into the congregation of the Lord; even to his tenth generation shall he not enter into the congregation of the Lord (Deut. 23:2).

The Lord is longsuffering, and of great mercy, forgiving iniquity and transgression, and by no means clearing the guilty, visiting the iniquity of the fathers

*upon the children unto the third and fourth genera-
tion* (Num. 14:18).

*Our fathers have sinned, and are not; and we have
borne their iniquities* (Lam. 5:7).

*Thou shewest lovingkindness unto thousands, and
recompensest the iniquity of the fathers into the
bosom of their children after them: the Great, the
Mighty God, the Lord of hosts, is His name...* (Jer.
32:18).

I took some time here to give you God's Word to prove the
point that God hates sin, and when we disobey and do not repent,
He will visit the iniquity of the fathers unto the third and fourth
generation until the sin is dealt with.

Okay, let me start by defining a *curse*. What is a curse? A *curse*,
in the passage above, is a judgment that God pronounces on a person and their family line for disobeying His commandments and
instructions that are listed in the Bible.

Once under a curse, doors are opened in your life for demons
to enter in. These demons will then begin their work of binding
you and affecting your life; they bring disease, torture, misery,
and destruction on you and your children until the curse is broken and lifted in Jesus Christ's name.

Right now it is very possible that you and your children
are under a curse as a result of either your own personal sins
that you committed in the past, or as a result of something
your parents or other ancestors did which violated God's laws
and commandments.

A common misconception is that once we are saved through Jesus Christ, all of our demons are cast out, all our curses are broken, and all our sicknesses are healed immediately, but the Word of God does not say this happens automatically.

> *But He was wounded for our transgressions, He was bruised for our iniquities: the chastisement of our peace was upon Him; and with His stripes we are healed* (Isa. 53:5).

Healing is available at the Cross through Jesus Christ, but how many fellow believers do you know who are depressed, battling sicknesses, battling cancer, and taking prescription meds for insomnia and anxiety? Why are they still being tormented? Why are they not healed?

Healing, deliverance from demons, being set free of curses, and receiving the blessings of God are all available to the believer as a result of Jesus Christ's sacrifice on the Cross of Calvary. But we must appropriate these promises by meeting the conditions set out in God's Word for us to receive them.

The promises of God are available to us as Christians, but we are called to forgive others who have hurt us, to confess personal and generational sins that have been committed and repent of them, and then we need to break generational curses in Jesus' name so we can be healed and set free.

Curses are very serious and can run in a family for three to four generations or longer, depending on the sin that was committed. An example is the curse of idolatry, which is worshiping other gods. If you or your ancestors ever went to a psychic, had their palms read, received or performed a tarot card reading, played with a Ouija board, participated in a séance, had a horoscope reading, studied astrology, tried to contact your dead relatives, water witched, got involved in Wicca, Freemasonry, Eastern Star, prayed to dead saints, or dabbled in witchcraft or the occult...these are examples of sins that will bring a three- to four-generational curse.

That means you are cursed, your children are cursed, your grandchildren are cursed, and your great-grandchildren are cursed by God until the curse is broken. Even worse, there are some curses that can run in a family for as many as ten generations, such as the "curse of the bastard," which is a result of conceiving a child outside of marriage.

> *A bastard shall not enter into the congregation of the Lord; even to his tenth generation shall he not enter into the congregation of the Lord* (Deut. 23:2).

Curses bring judgment on a person and their family line and open the doors for demons to enter in and begin their work to kill, steal, and destroy until the curses are dealt with and broken.

A red flag that you may be under a curse is if there is a particular sickness or other problem you are dealing with, and the same thing was experienced by your parent or a grandparent.

Now God says in His Word in Deuteronomy 11:26-28:

> *Behold, I set before you this day a blessing and a curse; A blessing, if ye obey the commandments of the Lord your God, which I command you this day: And a curse, if ye will not obey the commandments of the Lord your God, but turn aside out of the way which I command you this day, to go after other gods, which ye have not known.*

So the choice ours—the blessing or the curse. If we obey God we will be blessed. If we disobey Him and His Word, we and our children will be judged and fall under a curse.

Let me repeat: curses are not automatically broken when we become saved. You can be saved and still be under a curse. In Galatians 6:7 the Word says: "Be not deceived; God is not mocked: for whatsoever a man soweth, that shall he also reap."

We can be set free by confessing and repenting of personal and generational sins, forgiving others, closing the doors to the demons, breaking the generational curses in Jesus's name, and finally casting out the demons that came in through the sin doorway.

In a few moments, I am going to take you through some prayers you can pray to break the generational curses, but before I do I want to cover a prerequisite for you being set free, and it is called *forgiveness*.

We *must* forgive everyone who has wronged us.

If we want to break curses and be blessed, if we want to be forgiven of our sins, if we want to be set free of the "tormentors" (demons), then we must forgive. This is not optional.

But you are thinking right now, "John, I was raped!" Or "John, you don't know what they did to me! They lied—they stabbed me in the back—they stole from me—they cheated on me. I can't forgive!"

It doesn't matter what was done to you in the past. If you do not forgive, then God will not forgive you, and the curse, the torment by demons, and the sicknesses will continue until you forgive!

There will be no relief for you or me if we do not forgive others.

Unforgiveness is the greatest blockage to deliverance and blessings and to God hearing and answering your prayers.

Take a look at these Scripture verses:

And forgive us our debts, as we forgive our debtors (Matt. 6:12).

But if ye forgive not men their trespasses, neither will your Father forgive your trespasses (Matt. 6:15).

Then came Peter to Him, and said, Lord, how oft shall my brother sin against me, and I forgive him? till seven times? Jesus saith unto him, I say not unto thee, Until seven times: but, Until seventy times seven. Therefore is the Kingdom of Heaven likened unto a certain king, which would take account of his servants. And when he had begun to reckon, one was brought unto him, which owed him ten thousand talents. But forasmuch as he had not to pay, his lord commanded him to be sold, and his wife, and children, and all that he had, and payment to be made. The servant therefore fell down, and worshipped him, saying, Lord, have patience with me, and I will pay thee all. Then the lord of that servant was moved with compassion, and loosed him, and forgave him the debt. But the same servant went out, and found one of his fellowservants, which owed him an hundred pence: and he laid hands on him, and took him by the throat, saying, Pay me that thou owest. And his fellowservant fell down at his feet, and besought him, saying, Have patience with me, and I will pay thee all. And he would not: but went and cast him into prison, till he should pay the debt. So when his fellowservants saw what was done, they were very sorry, and came and told unto their lord all that was done. Then his lord, after that he had called him, said unto him, O thou wicked servant, I forgave thee all that debt, because thou desiredst me: Shouldest not thou also have had compassion on thy fellowservant, even as I had pity on thee? And his lord was wroth, and delivered him to the tormentors, till he should pay all that was due unto him. So likewise shall my heavenly Father do also unto you, if ye from your hearts forgive not every one his brother their trespasses (Matt. 18:21-35).

And when ye stand praying, forgive, if ye have ought against any: that your Father also which is in Heaven may forgive you your trespasses. But if ye do not forgive, neither will your Father which is in Heaven forgive your trespasses (Mark 11:25-26).

For we know him that hath said, Vengeance belongeth unto Me, I will recompense, saith the Lord. And again, The Lord shall judge His people (Heb. 10:30).

Do you really want to hang onto unforgiveness and hold on to the demons and continue being tormented? Of course not! So make a decision today to forgive.

Prayer to Forgive Others

Father God, in Jesus Christ's name I confess that I have held in my heart unforgiveness, bitterness, and resentment toward other people in my lifetime.

I am asking You to help me to forgive them, and right now in Jesus Christ's name I do now forgive the following people:

[speak the person's name whether living or dead]

I ask You, Father God, to pour out Your goodness, mercy, and grace on them, and bless and save them, in Jesus Christ's name.

I also now forgive and accept myself in Jesus Christ's name.

Because of Jesus Christ we have victory over curses and demons.

Christ hath redeemed us from the curse of the law, being made a curse for us: for it is written, Cursed is every one that hangeth on a tree: That the blessing of Abraham might come on the Gentiles through Jesus Christ; that we might receive the promise of the Spirit through faith (Gal. 3:13-14).

If we confess our sins, He is faithful and just to forgive us our sins, and to cleanse us from all unrighteousness (1 John 1:9).

How then do we break curses? By confessing the sin and asking the Lord Jesus Christ to forgive you and/or your ancestors involved in the sin. You then renounce the curse and close the door to it, break the curse in Jesus Christ's name and command the demons to come out of you in His name. Next release the blessing.

Let's take action and break the curse.

Prayer to Break Generational Curses

Father God, in Jesus Christ's name I confess that Jesus Christ is Lord.

Lord Jesus, I confess and believe that You died for me and my sins, and that You rose again from the dead and are seated at the right hand of the Father.

Lord Jesus, You paid the price for me that I might be redeemed from the curse and enter into the blessing.

Father God, in Jesus Christ's name I confess that, in the past, I and my ancestors have broken Your laws and commandments and that this has brought a curse on me and my family.

I confess all sins back to the very first thought, word, deed, and gesture that I or my ancestors have committed: Sins of idolatry, pride, sexual sins of fornication and adultery, incest, rape, the murder of the unborn (abortion), dishonoring of parents, involvement in witchcraft and the occult, membership in secret societies, having children outside of marriage, cursing Israel, racism toward other ethnic groups, not helping the poor, robbing You of tithes and offerings, not coming to the help of the Lord, and anything else known or unknown that I or my ancestors have done.

[Mention anything else you or your ancestors have done that God brings to your mind and specifically name it. Examples: Going to a psychic or fortune teller, using a Ouija board or tarot cards, reading horoscopes or studying astrology, involvement in Wicca, Reiki, yoga, the martial arts, or other means to tell the future.]

I now renounce Satan and all of his demons, all personal and ancestral contact with the occult, and I put you on notice, Satan, that I hate you and your demons and want nothing more to do with you.

Father God, in Jesus Christ's name I repent and renounce all of our sins that I and my ancestors have committed, and I ask you to forgive me and my family, in Jesus Christ's name.

In Jesus's name I now close all doors opened to the demons thru these sins, and I lay claim to Galatians 3:13: "Christ hath redeemed us from the curse of the law, being made a curse for us: for it is written, Cursed is every one that hangeth on a tree...."

*I now **break** and **loose** myself and my descendants from all personal and generational curses, and I lift the curses, in Jesus's name.*

In Jesus Christ's name I also break and cancel all blood oaths, contracts, covenants, rituals, pacts and agreements made with the devil and his demons by me or by my ancestors and command the curses and every associated demon to loose me now and come out of me and my children and go to where the Lord Jesus Christ is sending you!

I now ask you, Father God, to fill me with the Holy Spirit and release on me and my children all the blessings of Abraham that I am entitled to through Christ Jesus and that me and my family might receive the promise of the Spirit through faith in Jesus Christ's name.

I will live and not die to declare the works of the Lord!

I can do all things through Christ Jesus which strengthens me.

Greater is He that is within me than He that is in the world.

I break all hexes, vexes, curses and spells, incantations, evil declarations, psychic prayers and thoughts, witchcraft control, mind control and lay lines, jinxes, juju, effigies, fetishes, bewitchments, and enchantments off of me in Jesus's name, and loose myself and my children from them in Jesus Christ's name.

Summary

How bad do you want your freedom, and how bad do you want to stay free? Now you have the tools to destroy what's holding you down.

.

CHAPTER ELEVEN

"I Am Dead"

Life is beautiful, but it has an end. One Sunday afternoon after church, I made plans with my best friend, David. We were excited to meet up and have the opportunity to see the greatest baseball game ever. We had waited for a very long time for this to happen. The best two teams were going to play against each other that afternoon. They were the best of their division, with the best record, and it was going to be a faceoff. The weather couldn't have been any more perfect than it was that afternoon: Mid-70s and blue sky, not even one cloud in the heavens.

David and I grew up together watching these two teams play, way back from childhood. I asked him to meet me by my house, as he lived within walking distance from my place. We were going to drive to the stadium in my car. We were amped up and fired up and ready to go. David was cool, easygoing, tall and slender, with jet-black hair and light brown eyes, and he enjoyed the gym. He had a charisma with the girls. I was medium built, with jet-black hair, dark brown eyes, and I loved working out.

David and I were inseparable and the best of friends. As he approached my house, I was waiting outside in front of my car. He yelled out, "Hey John, how's it going today? Are you ready to see your team lose?" I laughed out loud. We got in my car. "I must say, John, you keep this car in mint condition, beautiful and shining. This is a great sports car."

As we headed down the road, I was so tempted to turn on my CD player and pump up my Christian music. But I felt a little uncomfortable doing that; you see, my best friend wasn't a Christian, so I didn't want to offend him. As I turned on the radio and was trying to tune to a station that would be OK, all I heard was David scream at the top of his lungs, saying "Watch out!" And then the world went dark.

What is life? What is its value? What price tag could you put on it? Why are we here? It's funny how we get a birth date, a place where we are born, and a time to die. But what happens in between these events? I heard once that as soon as we are born, we start to die. In the meantime, we grow up, go to school, travel, make friends, make career choices, and get a job. Many people choose marriage, while a few remain single.

Life is a journey. We know that the station where we get on the train of life is called the birthplace, the hospital. As we travel through life on this train, we pass many stops, circumstances, situations, and opportunities, but we never know where and when will be the final stop.

[There is a] *time to weep, and a time to laugh; a time to mourn, and a time to dance* (Eccles. 3:4).

As I opened my eyes, not having a recollection of where I was, I found myself surrounded by doctors and nurses. As I tried so hard to put the pieces together, I realized that I was in the intensive care unit of a hospital. I heard the voice of the doctor; he reassured me that everything was going to be OK. But in a flash I remembered my dear friend, David. As I turned to the doctor, in a small whisper I asked, "How is my friend David?"

The doctor bowed his head and in a gentle voice said, "Your friend didn't make it. He passed away." There was a cry in my spirit, knowing that David wasn't a Christian. That night I fell into a deep sleep because of the medications given to me, and I had a vivid dream. In that dream, I was in my house. It was a beautiful day, and as I stared out my living room window I saw the mailman approaching the house.

I jumped out of my recliner and ran to the door, down the three steps of the house, and to the mailbox to get the mail. As I shuffled through the letters I saw a light bill, a phone bill, my mortgage, and in between there was an unusual envelope, an envelope like I had never seen before and with very unusual writing on it. All it said on the envelope was, "A letter from your best friend, David." My hands started to shake as I opened the letter. My breath was heavy, and worry and fear came over me. This is what I read:

Dear Best Friend,

I hope this letter finds you well. As for me, I wish I could say the same. I find myself in a place where you can't count the days or the time, the months or the years. I was given this one opportunity to write you this letter. Here goes. Why, why, why? We grew up together, we denied each other nothing, we wore each other's clothes, we went to the same elementary school together, we skipped over to junior high school together, and we landed in high school. We shared many classes throughout our education, we knew each other's best secrets, but there was only one great secret that you kept from me. His name is Jesus Christ.

Why, why, why, did you keep this one secret from me? I thought that you loved me as your best friend. Now I find myself in a place that words can't even describe. A forever place of no rest, sadness, sorrow, grief, torment, torture, and, all along, you knew about this place and you kept this away from me, the truth. Who would have known if you had shared your faith with me, like you shared everything else with me? As I write this letter to you, my tormentors are waiting for me. These are my final words to you, my dear friend. You were a Christian, and yet you kept the best from me. Were you embarrassed; were you ashamed? Why would you do this to me? I could have had Jesus in my life, but look at me now. Farewell forever; I will never see you again. The tormentors are waiting for me.

Summary

How is your evangelism to the dead world that we live in today? Are you ashamed of the Gospel, or are you living for Christ? Are you a mouthpiece for Jesus Christ, or has the devil shut you down? Are you standing on the tomb of the dead and calling people out, or are you just passing them by? We are called to sound the trumpet. My question is, does your trumpet have the sound of Jesus Christ?

CHAPTER TWELVE

The Letter

This is one of the hardest letters I will probably ever write in this lifetime. I thank God for my salvation, for all that He has done for me, and for the ministry He has given me—but such a heavy responsibility it is to carry. The spiritual warfare I go through at times is beyond human comprehension, even to the point that other believers can't believe it. Yet one thing I have learned is to trust and stand on God's Word and His promises.

Sometimes I feel like the Old Testament prophet Jeremiah, that somehow God has deceived me. I thought Christianity meant to get saved, buy a Bible, and go to church. Never in my life would I have thought that I would have a ministry. Ministry starts with holy character, brokenness, and giving of yourself for others. After dealing with demons for twenty-five years on the other side, I never wanted to sign up to have a deliverance ministry. I have struggled and fought with God to accept this ministry.

One of my first radio interviews was with Omegaman Radio, hosted by Shannon Davis, to share my testimony. He made a comment about me having a deliverance ministry, and inside myself I was thinking, *This guy has it all wrong.* He would mail me deliverance CDs and DVDs, and I would put them on my kitchen table and try to forget about them. From time to time, Shannon would ask me if I had the opportunity to listen to them. I would say, "I'm so close to listening to them that I can touch them," but my heart was far from touching anything that had to do with deliverance ministry. All I wanted to do was go to church, read my Bible, and make it to Heaven.

Again, I felt like Jeremiah, called into a calling I never asked for and surely didn't want. But God doesn't always tell us everything up front; otherwise, we may never say yes to Him or do anything that has to do with the kingdom. Please don't misunderstand me. I have no regrets. Since the first day that God called me, my life has been an amazing journey. And as I share my personal thoughts with you from my heart, one thing I know is that I will never quit or give up. I'm in it to the very end. I have found my place in life that no college, nor anything of the world can give me, but only Jesus—and I thank Him every day for stopping and looking my way.

I met the grace and mercy of God in 1999, and I stand on this Scripture, Jeremiah 29:11-13:

> *For I know the thoughts that I think toward you, says the Lord, thoughts of peace and not of evil, to give*

you a future and a hope. Then you will call upon Me and go and pray to Me, and I will listen to you. And you will seek Me and find Me, when you search for Me with all your heart (NKJV).

One of the hardest things the devil hits me with, or tries to remind me of, is the cruelty of my previous life and the damage I caused to believers and nonbelievers through witchcraft. I get precious emails every day from believers around the world who are being tormented beyond measure. These are Christian brothers and sisters who love the Lord dearly and are being attacked by the hosts of hell. I say this with a broken heart: Where is the spiritual warfare Church today?

I truly believe the Church of Jesus Christ is going back its roots, back to the Book of Acts, the way it began—casting out devils, healing the sick, and getting people saved. I thank God every day that in 1999, in my own innocent way as a young believer, I signed a piece of paper. I wrote: "I'm doing a life sentence in Jesus Christ, and I want no parole." I don't believe in backsliding. Backsliding is a choice. Once you say yes to Jesus Christ you have been enlisted in the most elite fighting force of any lifetime, and there is no turning back.

I am so grateful for everything God has done for me. I am indebted to the Cross of Jesus Christ, and it's time to fight. It's amazing that our Lord and Savior would remove someone who was so deep into the vows of witchcraft, clean him up, sanctify him with His blood, and fill him with His Spirit to then unleash him with the power of the Holy Spirit, to wage war against the very kingdom of darkness that he believed, trusted, and served for twenty-five years. I love my Jesus. He has the greatest sense of humor that I have ever seen in my life.

Many times when I preach somewhere or visit a conference or event, people who don't know me manifest with demons out of nowhere and start to scream, "John Ramirez, we hate you and are going to destroy you! Why did you leave us?" When these things happen, I'm humbled, and I thank God once more that in 1999, out of the community where I lived, among 179 buildings, Jesus knew my address. What an amazing God we serve! No regrets; I love You, Jesus, forever! Thank You for giving me a life with purpose. Now I have a destiny, all because Jesus decided to look my way.

Sincerely,

EVANGELIST JOHN RAMIREZ

BONUS MATERIAL

Out of the Devil's Cauldron

Introduction and Chapter 1

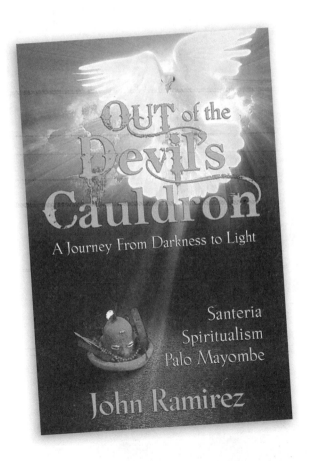

Mark of the Beast

Shifting my feet to fight the cold, I waited at the busy crosswalk and watched my breath disperse like smoke in the wintry air. Though the temperature hovered in the low-20s, the main street through Castle Hill in the Bronx teemed with people as it always did this time of day. A cluster of little kids played at the curb, seemingly unaware of the traffic roaring past them just a few yards away. Someone leaned on their car horn and shouted obscenities at another driver. A police car zigzagged through traffic, its siren blaring and bleeping to make a path through the crush of vehicles. *Home sweet home,* I thought cynically. The light changed.

"Hey, John! What's happenin'?" a voice shouted.

I looked up to see a man I recognized from Step-In, the corner bar near the train station, leaning against the door of the barbershop. "Not much, man. Just keepin' it cool," I replied. We slapped hands in passing before I quickly turned the corner down a side street, not wanting to make small talk.

The cold wind whipping through Castle Hill hit me full in the face, and I turned up the collar of my wool coat. Though the winter chill invigorated me physically, something nagged at my mind—a troubled feeling I couldn't shake. I glanced up to see an older Hispanic woman outside her storefront staring at me, and as I turned my dark, piercing eyes on her, fear swept over her countenance. She made the sign of the cross and hurried inside, a bell jingling in her wake.

Go to your aunt's house. The same thought I'd had earlier that day came again, this time more insistent. By now it was unmistakable: the spirits were speaking to me. *Go to your aunt's house.* I considered not going, but only for a minute. Changing directions, I looped back the way I'd come but avoided the main street, arriving at Aunt Maria's three-story clapboard house within minutes. I rang the doorbell and waited, then rang it again. After the third ring I decided she must not be home, but something told me to go knock on the basement door. Stepping through the chain-link gate that accessed the basement entry, I started to knock when I saw that the door was already cracked open. I walked in.

Eerie vibes filled the room—vibes I knew well—and instantly I realized some sort of witchcraft ritual was in process. Through the dark I saw my aunt, a man, and another woman sitting at a *mesa blanca*, a "white table" used for witchcraft readings. I glanced at the floor in front of the table and saw strange symbols written in chalk with lighted candles on them, making it appear as if the floor were on fire. For the first time I got a good look at the man sitting behind the table. Short and stocky, he wore a bandana around his head like a biker, and his medium-length black hair was matched by coal-black eyes that seemed to pierce right through me. Whoever he was, I could tell he was in charge of this gathering, and his mysterious aura was strangely beckoning.

My aunt waved me over, not wanting to interrupt the reading. As the reading went on, I stared at the symbols on the floor, fascinated by the power and heaviness that hung like a lead cloak over the room. Witchcraft was no stranger to me—I had been casting spells and growing to new levels of power since I was ten years old—but the energy coming off this man was like nothing I'd ever felt before. Whatever it was, I wanted it too.

I listened as he described the different aspects of this religion until finally my curiosity won out.

"Hey, what's going on?" I whispered to Aunt Maria.

"This is Palo Mayombe," she replied in a monotone, tucking a strand of her salt-and-pepper hair back under her white bandana. As she said that, the man turned to me and opened his mouth to speak. My heart thumped like a jackhammer in my chest when I heard the words of his prophecy.

"This young man is your right hand and most faithful person in the occult," he said to my aunt. He held my eyes for a long moment, letting the words sink in. "He is a very powerful warlock who will become a major player in the religion. He must be in the first group of new initiates next month because of his power and commitment to Palo Mayombe."

Aunt Maria's eyes widened with awe, and I watched as a slow smile spread across her face. In that instant we both knew I had just walked into a supernatural appointment—her nephew was about to become a major power player, controlling spiritual regions of the Bronx.

That afternoon was a turning point for me. I knew I was going to another level in the spirit realm and would have power like I never knew before.

Contract with the Devil

The priesthood ceremony took place two weeks later in the basement of Aunt Maria's house. As I approached the house on foot, I could feel the rhythm of the conga drums vibrating on the night air. The sound of chanting inside told me that those who came to watch the ceremony—seasoned priests of the religion—were beckoning the spirits, setting the spiritual atmosphere for what would take place on that night in February 1997.

Opening the basement door ushered me into a world few people will ever experience. My aunt's basement had been transformed into a ritualistic chamber, dressed for a serious witchcraft ceremony. Flickering candles cast mysterious shadows on the walls, and seventeen tree branches covered the floor, one for each of the initiates to sit on. Two or three dozen roosters squawked from a makeshift cage in the corner of the room. I knew what they were for.

The music got louder and the songs more intense, with lyrics inviting the devil to come as the hours ticked toward midnight. Somebody asked the helpers to bring us into another part of the basement, and we stood shoulder to shoulder in front of what

I sensed to be an altar. I felt the presence of demons so thick I could almost touch it. When the drumbeats reached their fullest a heavy presence beyond human comprehension descended on the room. Even though the words chanted were African and Spanish, I knew in my heart and soul and spirit they were summoning the devil.

It was *Nafumbe*, the devil himself.

Beads of sweat broke out on my forehead, and a strange mix of terror and excitement swelled within me. At five minutes to midnight, the high *tata* priest stood in front of me and started chanting some words, spelling out the contract that was about to take place. He chose me to go first. Taking a one-edged razor, he cut into my flesh. As my blood ran, I knew the contract was being initiated.

Out of the seventeen initiates that night, the devil chose only me to be initiated as *tata*, the calling of a high priest. The godfather cut a pentagram into the flesh of my right arm, distinguishing me from the others. The priests boasted about how seldom one is singled out for the calling of *tata*, and I held my head high: I had the mark of the beast on my body.

Early the next morning I woke up, bloody and swollen from the night's ritual, and made my way to the bathroom. It was still dark out and very quiet, but I could tell from the single small window in the basement that dawn would come soon. I flipped the switch to turn on the light and leaned in close to peer at my reflection in the mirror.

The face that stared back at me was the face of a new person, a new man. The black eyes that gazed from the reflection were eyes I had never seen before: I had been born into Palo Mayombe to be a *Palero tata*—a high priest.

CHAPTER
ONE

Beginnings

My blood boiling with rage, I walked into a bar and scanned the smoky room for my father, knowing he had to be here. Where else would he be when he was not at home or driving his gypsy cab? And there he was, just as I expected—sitting on a barstool, leaning in close to a woman with dark hair in a tight blouse. He was smiling and laughing, and I knew thoughts of my mother were far from his mind.

A movement across the room caught my eye. A man I'd never seen before glared at my father and clenched his fists. Even from this distance I could feel a thick vibe of jealousy and anger radiating from him.

The strange man reached inside his coat, and in that moment I realized what he was about to do—what I had secretly wanted somebody to do for a long time: kill my father.

Two shots rang out, and as my father slumped to the wooden floor, the stranger crossed the room to pump the rest of the bullets in the barrel into his cold, vile heart. While my dad lay dying, the bullet holes still smoking, I stepped from behind the stranger and stared down at my father's face. His eyes grew wide, and as his soul's silver cord was snapping I told him all he needed to do was show some love and concern for his wife and family. Just a little. Then his firstborn son would not have spent so many days and nights of his young life wishing his father was dead and finally seeing it come true.

The last words he heard me say were: "I wish it had been me who pulled the trigger instead."

—␍␊—

The wail of a siren jarred me from sleep, and I sat bolt upright in bed, shaking in a cold sweat. *A dream...it was only a dream.* The same one I'd had over and over again since my father's murder the year I turned thirteen. I looked over at my brothers, snoring softly through the uproar of the South Bronx streets outside our dingy apartment window. The room was freezing as usual, but I was used to it. Unable to sleep, I crossed to the window and peered out. A couple of neighborhood thugs huddled over a trashcan fire on the corner, and a second police car roared down the street, its sirens chasing after the first one that had awakened me from the cruel dream.

How did I get here? I wondered. I was born in Puerto Rico but grew up in the Bronx as the oldest of four sons. From the

Caribbean island of Puerto Rico, with its glorious sunshine, palm trees, warm breezes, and crystal waters, we moved to the harsh, cold streets of the South Bronx. As a child, I would fold my arms on an open windowsill on one of the upper floors of our apartment building and look out at the trash-cluttered sea of concrete, glass, and brick buildings. I had an artistic soul, even as a boy, but for miles into the horizon I saw no art or beauty. All I saw was an ocean of ugliness.

Goodhearted by nature, I was a spirited child who did my best to help my mother and brothers out. I knew my mother loved me, and that was very important, but what I craved most was my father's approval and love. It was something every growing boy needed. I longed for a dad to participate in my life, to say he was proud of me and that he loved me. It was something I never got.

Instead my absentee father had countless women on the side, bar fights, and drunken rages. His insane exploits ensnared him and saddened us deeply. I felt seething resentment even at a young age that he cheated us of a normal family's prosperity, blessings, and happiness.

His careless, cruel behavior toward my mother and our family became more horrible with each passing year. I would go from being a kind boy to being a very angry one. As time went on, my feelings and outlook on the world festered with the bitterness I felt. Eventually my once-kind heart turned stone cold.

The Bittersweet Big Apple

My mother, Esther Martinez, was only a sweet sixteen-year-old when she married Eustaquio Ramirez in Santurce, Puerto

Rico, and gave birth to me that same year in December 1963. The very next year she gave birth to my brother Julio. We stayed in Rio Piedras, Puerto Rico, for one year until my parents and both sides of their families came to the United States.

Upon arriving in America, in rapid succession my brothers George and Eustaquio Jr. came along. But the challenges grew deeper. As I got older I realized our family had not been prepared for the realities of living in New York.

This was supposed to be the start of a better life in the most promising city in the world—New York. Manhattan was the island that was so close, yet from where we lived in the South Bronx, it seemed a world away. It often felt like we were trapped in a time warp. We lived in an apartment prison with invisible bars that caged us in an endless, living nightmare.

The reality in which we lived seemed like a bad dream. My father, who was supposed to take the lead, instead was constantly running out of the home and out of our lives. He was missing in action for most of our lives. But when he did park the gypsy cab he drove for a living, we'd hear his keys jingle in the lock and he'd swing the front door open to step back into our lives. "Papi's home!" one of my younger brothers would yell. My dad was a young and handsome man with piercing eyes and thick black hair. Within seconds, bustling in her housedress and ever-present apron, my mother would put away any anger because of his absence, and her heart would be taken in again just by the sight of him.

He'd stroll into the kitchen for a bite to eat as though he had never left.

"What's the matter with these sons of mine?" he complained to my mom, pointing his finger at us as we stood in the doorway between the tiny living room and the cramped kitchen.

"They're good boys, Eustaquio. What do you mean?" my mother said, stirring a pot of yellow rice on the stove.

"If they were good boys they would ask for my blessing whenever they see me on the street like their cousins do," my father said. "'Bendicion, Tio!' they always say, but do my own sons ever ask me to bless them? No—all they ever want is a dollar so they can go buy candy." He glared in my direction, assuming that as the oldest I spoke for all four of us boys. Bitterness and hatred churned in my heart. I knew that a reply of any kind was useless. And then my father would make his way to the living room, fall out on the sofa in a drunken stupor, and go to sleep.

Often the next morning, although we were his own family, he seemed so detached, like his mind was elsewhere. It was as if he needed to be treated more like visiting royalty than a father, and we all tiptoed around and tried our best to please him and make him part of our lives.

My mother probably wanted to tell him news of her last few days or weeks. My brothers and I were bursting to share our baseball victories or basketball stories or talk about what happened in or after school. Maybe mention some cool car we saw or some girl we had a crush on, or even share a funny joke we heard. But more often than not we just ate in relative silence, afraid to say much of anything.

There seemed to be a gateless fence with barbed wire around him that we were afraid to scale, knowing we'd get cut. At other times it seemed more like a brick wall that we could never break through where he kept his emotions walled in, never expressing any real joy or love for us.

I never knew who my father really was and wondered if he even liked us, but I couldn't figure out why not. I saw other boys with their fathers going to the park, hitting a ball, playing catch, talking about sports. Those fathers would talk enthusiastically with them, pat them on the back, and walk along with their sons, sharing a good laugh. I yearned for that kind of relationship, but no matter what I tried he'd just push me away and call me "stupid." Some words are shattering to a child, and stupid is certainly one of them.

My father didn't seem to care that his dysfunction was so damaging. He seemed to go out of his way to discourage my brothers and me, to criticize us and talk to us in a condescending tone. We were never good enough to make him happy. And I swore I'd never be like him when I became a father and a man. I hated who he was, and I was even ashamed to tell others he was my dad.

Every now and then I held out hope that he would look at me and it would spark a glimmer of affection—in that moment he'd remember the little boy he once was. Or he'd want me to look up to him as the man I would one day become, but he left no positive impressions. The picture was either distorted or ugly or strangely blank. He left no template for me to pour myself into, no image for me to model myself after.

He frequently made promises, and like fools we let our hopes get high.

"Hey, John," he would call from the sofa, a beer in his hand. "This weekend, once my shift is over, I'll take you and your brothers to Coney Island. What do you say to that, huh?"

His smile looked so genuine I believed him. "Want to go to the amusement park? Obey your mother all week and we'll go do the rides on Saturday."

But Saturday would come and my father was nowhere to be found. He had run out of our lives once again, to be missing for days or weeks on end.

Mom was the backbone of the family. With four children at a very young age, it was difficult for her to do things and move around from place to place. Since my mother was poorly educated and had no work experience outside the home, we depended on public assistance, food stamps, and whatever help my mother could get. Everything ran out after only a week or two, but we tried to make the best of it. From time to time my father would give her twenty dollars to buy food for the week. Even back then, that was not enough.

But at times it was much worse than that. Once I walked into the kitchen and stopped cold, staring in amazement at the five dollars he had left on the counter for food and other necessities. Five dollars! For his wife and family of four growing boys! Even with my grade school math I knew that five people (six whenever he came back home), divided by five dollars, meant my dad had left less than a dollar apiece for each of us to live on for the week. I also knew that even in the late '60s and early '70s that was no money. My mother used the basics—rice, beans, and potatoes—to stretch everything. But even with her creative and good cooking, five dollars was just a bad joke. What my father had left for us to survive on was more of an insult than a help.

"Five dollars! You know that's not enough to feed a family," my mother pleaded, her brow creased with worry lines.

"Then maybe you should put the five dollars in some water and stretch it," my father called back over his shoulder, a sneer on his face as he laughed at his joke. That was one of the many ways he humiliated my mother and controlled the family, by leaving us in lack.

Where Are You, God?

Like so many others, my father was involved in *espiritismo* (spiritualism) and appealed to his gods in a darkened room with strange rituals, chanting, and candles. To him it was just a cultural thing. One afternoon toward dusk I walked down the hall of our apartment and heard my father chanting in the bedroom he shared with my mother. Tiptoeing to the door, I peeked through the crack and saw him before a makeshift altar glowing with candles. The sight of my father chanting to his favorite saint, whom he called *San Lazaro* (St. Lazarus), both frightened and fascinated me.

He often sent me with five dollars to the nearby botanica, a potion store, to buy an orange candle and flowers for San Lazaro, whom he probably loved more than his own kids. I could still hear his words throbbing in my mind: "Hurry and don't lose the money!" I would run down the stairs like a bat out of hell, trying to catch my breath and running past the people sitting on the front stoop. I was on a mission, dashing through cars in heavy traffic, my hands tightly gripped on the money. As I ran into the botanica, I hoped and prayed they would have what my dad sent me to buy. If they didn't, he would be disappointed—and angry with me.

Unlike many other Hispanic families, my family never went to the big Catholic church in our neighborhood, but I had seen the crucifixes and pictures of Jesus and heard people call Him "God." If He was God, why didn't He show up in my life? Why did He allow my brothers and me to hurt at the hands of our own father—not to mention the anguish my mother endured? I pushed the thoughts aside as quickly as they came. It was too painful to dwell on what the answer might be.

One afternoon I went down the block to play in the school-yard, but to my surprise I heard loud music emanating from it. Curious to see what all the commotion was about, I drew nearer and saw a large red tent with a church service going on under-neath. Somebody was playing a keyboard, and a choir swayed at the back of the tent as they belted out songs about Jesus. For a while I stood at a distance, touched by the music and stirred up in my heart. I couldn't put my finger on it, but instinctively I knew something very special was going on in this place. While the choir sang, a man came around off the stage and touched people on the forehead randomly. Whenever he touched them, they fell to the ground onto their backs, as if going to sleep. They looked so peaceful lying there, and suddenly I wanted the same thing to happen to me. I felt a love there that was indescribable.

As if on cue, the man leading the event started moving in my direction. My pulse quickened. One by one he touched peo-ple in the crowd near me, the closest one being a man standing right next to me. The man fell out on his back, and I could see the blessing on him—that something special I longed for too. I looked up expectantly, waiting for the minister to touch me, but he had passed me by, moving to another section of the crowd instead. I left that event feeling heartbroken, unwanted, and unloved. Why couldn't it be me they prayed for? Why couldn't it be me they touched? The answer that flickered through my mind: I guess God doesn't love me either.

My Father, My Enemy

Most nights my father came home already roaring drunk and enflamed by rage. For no reason at all, or any feeble excuse, he would beat my mother. My brothers and I cowered in our rooms, trembling with fear. We were all just little boys, and I would bite my lip and beg God to make the screaming and hitting stop.

One night the sound of my mother screaming pulled me out of a deep sleep. I leaped from the top bunk bed where I slept and stumbled down the hallway, my stomach churning in knots. As I approached the kitchen, the sound of shattering glass exploded in the air. My dad had come home drunk—at two o'clock in the morning—and demanded the meal my mother always had waiting for him.

"You good-for-nothing woman! I don't know why I put up with you!" he yelled, looking for something else to throw. My mother sobbed as she tried to serve him the dinner she spent all afternoon cooking. Suddenly a reheated meal of beans, rice, tomatoes, chicken, and plantains went airborne as he slammed his dinner plate against the wall.

"Eustaquio, nooo!" my mother wailed. I watched my father's face—her reaction flipped a switch in his drunken brain and unleashed a monster.

He grabbed her by the hair and began to beat her mercilessly. At one point during his pounding, my mother—literally knocked out of her shoes by him—managed to break away and run barefoot in terror down the hall into their bedroom. She struggled to lock the door in a futile effort to escape him. He lunged after her and broke down the door, and her screams grew louder as the beating continued. Though I was still a young boy, I knew I had to rescue her. I bolted into the room and jumped on my dad's back to stop him from hurting my mother. He turned around, eyes blazing with fire, cursed me, and tore me off him with rough hands, throwing me violently across the room. I hit the floor hard in a broken heap, feeling physically and emotionally hurt, angry, and powerless as he continued to beat my mother.

Finally, at four o'clock in the morning, his rage spent, my father passed out and the house returned to its now-eerie quiet. Shaking with fear and anger, I crawled back into my bunk bed and tried to go to sleep. In just three hours I would have to wake up, get dressed, and go to school as if nothing had happened. I would have to show a brave face to the world, pretending that my home life was not the living hell it truly was.

That night as I examined my bruises and thought about the injuries my mother must have too, my hatred for my father grew stronger. It was that night I first wished my father was dead. I didn't realize it then, but one day my wish would come true.

A Playbook to the Enemy's Tactics...

While much of the Church sleeps, dark forces from the underworld are being unleashed with increasing violence and perversion. Yet God stands prepared to display His awesome deliverance and transforming power through a remnant of Christ-followers who know they are called to kick in the gates of hell.

John Ramirez is living proof that you can go to hell and back. A former high priest of a New York-based satanic cult, he wreaked havoc on unsuspecting people for years before he had a supernatural encounter with Jesus Christ and broke free from Satan's kingdom.

Unmasking the Devil is an eye-opening primer that provides firsthand accounts of how Satan's army works. John teaches believers how to arm themselves with the power of the Holy Spirit to destroy the works of darkness in their lives.

John Ramirez is a watchman on the wall for such a time as this. In his first book, *Out of the Devil's Cauldron*, he told the chilling story of how he was groomed to be a high-ranking priest in Santeria, spiritualism, and the occult.

John's passion for setting people free continues in *Unmasking the Devil: Spiritual Warfare—Patterns and Cycles of the Underworld*. Within these pages he exposes the works of darkness on a greater level, giving believers a "playbook" to the enemy's game tactics.

"Spiritual warfare is a must for every Christian if they are going to survive in the coming years," says John Ramirez. *"It's time to stop playing patty-cake with the devil and learn how to put hell on notice."*

About the Author

John Ramirez is an international evangelist, author, and speaker. For sixteen years he has been teaching believers from the Virgin Islands to Germany and on TV shows such as *The 700 Club,* TBN, The Word Network, and The Church Channel how to defeat the enemy. If you are interested in having John speak at your church or appear on one of your media shows, contact him at www.JohnRamirez.org.

Get — FREE E-BOOKS every week!

LOVE to READ club

JOIN *the* CLUB

As a member of the **Love to Read Club,** receive exclusive offers for FREE, 99¢ and $1.99 e-books* every week. Plus, get the **latest news** about upcoming releases from **top authors** like these...

DESTINYIMAGE.COM/FREEBOOKS

T.D. JAKES

BILL JOHNSON

CINDY TRIMM

JIM STOVALL

BENI JOHNSON

MYLES MUNROE

LOVE to READ club

DESTINY IMAGE